SpringerBriefs in Environment, Security, Development and Peace

Migration Studies

Volume 16

Series editor

Hans Günter Brauch

For further volumes:
http://www.springer.com/series/11825
http://www.afes-press-books.de/html/SpringerBriefs_ESDP_MiS.htm

Suwattana Thadaniti · Supang Chantavanich
Editors

The Impact of Displaced People's Temporary Shelters on Their Surrounding Environment

Springer

Chulalongkorn University

INSTITUTE OF ASIAN STUDIES
CHULALONGKORN UNIVERSITY

Asian Research Center for Migration

Editors
Suwattana Thadaniti
Social Research Institute
Chulalongkorn University
Bangkok
Thailand

Supang Chantavanich
Asian Research Center for Migration
Chulalongkorn University
Bangkok
Thailand

ISSN 2193-3162 ISSN 2193-3170 (electronic)
ISBN 978-3-319-02841-5 ISBN 978-3-319-02842-2 (eBook)
DOI 10.1007/978-3-319-02842-2
Springer Cham Heidelberg New York Dordrecht London

Library of Congress Control Number: 2013951795

Printed on acid-free paper

Springer is part of Springer Science+Business Media (www.springer.com)

Other Books by the Asian Research Center for Migration Chulalongkorn University Bangkok, Thailand in this Book Series Published by Springer

Yongyuth Chalamwong, Naruemon Thabchumpon and Supang Chantavanich, (Eds.): *Temporary Shelters and Surrounding Communities—Livelihood Opportunities, the Labour Market, Social Welfare and Social Security*. SpringerBriefs in Environment, Security, Development and Peace, vol. 15–Migration Studies Subseries No. 2 (Cham–Heidelberg–Dordrecht–London–New York: Springer-Verlag, 2014).

Premjai Vungsiriphisal, Dares Chusri and Supang Chantavanich (Eds.): *Humanitarian Assistance for Displaced Persons from Myanmar—Royal Thai Government Policy and Donor, INGO/NGO and UN Agency Delivery*. SpringerBriefs in Environment, Security, Development and Peace, vol. 17–Migration Studies Subseries No. 4 (Cham–Heidelberg–Dordrecht–London–New York: Springer-Verlag, 2014).

Ben HarkinsandSupang Chantavanich (Eds.) in cooperation with Nawita Direkwut and Aungkana Kamonpetch: *Resettlement of Displaced Persons on the Thai-Myanmar Border*. SpringerBriefs in Environment, Security, Development and Peace, vol. 18–Migration Studies Subseries No. 5 (Cham–Heidelberg–Dordrecht–London–New York: Springer-Verlag, 2014).

Acknowledgments

This book is based on a report by a research team organised by the Asian Research Center for Migration (ARCM) at Chulalongkorn University in Bangkok, Thailand. The research team would like to express gratitude to the Royal Thai Government for its cooperation and assistance with this research. We would also like to sincerely thank all of those who agreed to be interviewed during this study, for taking the time to share with us their insights and experiences related to the impact of displaced people's temporary shelters on their surrounding environment. We would also like to thank Dr. Supang Chantavanich and the Staff of the Asian Research Center for Migration for their assistance and support during the research.

The Editors would like to express their sincere thanks to the best and effective team of research assistants. They are Mr. Worawat Junthasi, Ms. Salila Trakulvech, Ms. Rewadee Chuckkasen, Ms. Pattama Chooprasert, Ms. Teenaranun Jaroenruanglert, Ms. Siriwan Ussavuschariyakul, Ms. Suthasinee Haruchaiyasak, Ms. Sawapa Tangsawapak, Ms. Sarisa Ungchomchoke, They were students of Kasetsart University and Chulalongkorn University.

Funding for this research was provided by UNDP. We would like to thank the Staff of UNDP and the Members of the United Nations inter-agency team for their generous support of this research.

We are hopeful that this report on the impact of displaced people's temporary shelters on their surrounding environment will be useful in providing more understanding and insights into the situation of displaced people in Thailand and will encourage every stakeholder to find a sustainable situation.

The Editors would like to thank the Language Editor Graham Bennett, the book series and Copy Editor PD Dr. Hans Günter Brauch, to Dr. Johanna Schwarz, Ms. Agata Oelschlaeger, Ms. Janet Sterritt of Springer's editorial office in Heidelberg, Germany and to Springer's book production team in Chennai in India. The Language Editor Graham Bennett, the book series and Copy Editor HGB, to Dr. Johanna Schwarz, Ms. Agata Oelschlaeger, Ms. Janet Sterritt of Springer's editorial office in Heidelberg, Germany and to Springer's book production team in Chennai in India.

The opinions expressed within this report are those of the research team alone and do not necessarily reflect the views of UNDP or EU.

Suwattana Thadaniti
Supang Chantavanich

Contents

Abbreviations

AFPFL	Anti-Fascist Peoples League
AMI	Aide Medicale Internationale
ARC	American Refugee Committee
ASEAN	Association of Southeast Asian Nations
BMS	Ban Mai Surin
CAL	Center for Applied Linguistics
CAN	Community Agriculture and Nutrition
CBNRM	Community-Based Natural Resource Management
CBO	Community-Based Organisation
CCSDPT	Committee for Coordination of Services to Displaced Persons in Thailand
COERR	Catholic Organisation for Emergency Relief and Refugees
CPA	Comprehensive Plan of Action
CPB	Communist Party of Burma
DAR	Development Assistance for Refugees
DFID	Department for International Development
DHS	Department of Homeland Security
DLI	Development through Local Integration
DP	Displaced Person
ECHO	European Commission Humanitarian Aid and Civil Protection
EFA	Education for All
EU	European Union
EUROPA	Official Website of European Commission
EVI	Extremely Vulnerable Individuals
ExCOM	Executive Committee of UNHCR
FAFA	Financial and Administrative Framework Agreement
FPA	Framework Partnership Agreement
GDP	Gross Domestic Product
GED	General Equivalency Diplomas
GIS	Geographical Information System
HIS	Health Information System

HIV	Human Immunodeficiency Virus
ICRC	International Committee of the Red Cross
IDP	Internally Displaced Person
IHL	International Humanitarian Law
ILO	International Labour Organisation
IOM	International Organisation for Migration
IPD	In-Patient Department
IRC	International Rescue Committee
IUCN	International Union for the Conservation of Nature
JFM	Joint Forest Management
JRS	Jesuit Refugee Service
KED	Karen Education Department
KEP	Karen Education Project
KHRG	Karen Human Rights Group
KnED	Karenni Education Department
KNPP	Karenni National Progressive Party
KNU	Karen National Union
KRC	Karen Refugee Committee
KSNG	Karen Student Network Group
KWO	Karen Women's Organisation
KYO	Karen Youth Organisation
LRRD	Linking Relief, Rehabilitation and Development
MCH	Maternal and Child Health
MOE	Ministry of Education
MOFA	Ministry of Foreign Affairs
MOI	Ministry of Interior
MRML	Mae Ra Ma Luang
NFE	Non-Formal Education
NGO	Non-Government Organisation
NLD	National League for Democracy
NSC	National Security Council
OCDP	Operation Center for Displaced Persons
OPD	Out Patient Department
OPE	Overseas Processing Entity
ORS	Oral Rehydration Salt
PAB	Provincial Admission Board
POC	Persons of Concern
PPAT	Planned Parenthood Association of Thailand
PRM	Bureau of Populations, Refugees and Migration
PVO	People's Volunteer Organisation
R & P	Reception and Placement Organisation
RTG	Royal Thai Government

SFP/TFP	Supplementary and Therapeutic Feeding Programs
SGBV	Sexual and Gender-Based Violence
SLORC	State Law and Order Restoration Council
SOPs	Standard Operation Procedures
SPDC	State Peace and Development Council
SSA	Shan State Army
SSS	Sugar Salt Solution
TB	Tuberculosis
TBBC	Thailand Burma Border Consortium
TDRI	Thailand Development Research Institute
THB	Thai Baht
UNHCR	United Nations High Commissioner for Refugees
UNICEF	The United Nations Children's Fund
VCT	Voluntary Counseling and Trading
VOLAGs	Voluntary Agencies
VSO	Voluntary Service Overseas
WE/C	World Education/Consortium
WEAVE	Women's Education for Advancement and Empowerment
WFP	United Nations World Food Programme
WWF	World Wide Fund for Nature
ZOA	ZOA Refugee Care

Executive Summary

This book presents an overview of environmental issues and impacts associated with displaced peoples' temporary shelters along the Thai–Myanmar border, with recommendations aimed at improving the environmental conditions in and around the settlements. Out of nine such temporary shelters, three were selected for detailed study: Ban Tham Hin in Ratchburi province, Ban Mai Nai Soi in Mae Hong Son province and Ban Mae La in Tak province. In each of these shelters, a variety of research methods was used to assess the environmental conditions, analyse displaced peoples' way of living and use of resources and document displaced peoples' perceptions of the environmental conditions they face. Data were collected by means of observation on field trips to each of the shelters, surveys, in-depth interviews, focus group meetings and desk research. Respondents included the displaced people themselves and staff members working in the shelter areas. Whenever relevant and possible, the scope of the research was not restricted to the shelters alone. Efforts were made to also assess environmental impacts produced by the presence of the shelters in the surrounding areas, by hearing officials and representatives from these areas in focus group meetings and through interviews.

The three temporary shelters examined are situated in sparsely populated, though not unpopulated, mountainous terrain, inside or nearby forest reserves. The mountains and forests are home to a variety of natural resources including wood and other vegetable materials, edibles and small rivers and creeks. Establishing temporary shelters for thousands or even tens of thousands displaced people in such areas are likely to cause environmental impacts, a thesis that is corroborated by the findings of this study.

The most important and consequential environmental issues and impacts appear to be those related to the use of resources available in the shelters' surroundings, and to the emission of solid and liquid wastes. The study found that the inhabitants of the temporary shelters collect a variety of resources found in the shelters' direct surroundings, including materials for the construction and maintenance of dwellings such as bamboo, hardwoods and leaves, edibles to supplement food rations supplied by the TBBC or as a livelihood strategy, materials used for cooking, and water. Such resources are not always collected in sustainable ways, and often in competition with the host communities.

There are several reasons why displaced people leave their settlements to forage in the surrounding areas. The RTG policy to only allow the use of non-durable materials in house construction results in the need for frequent replacement of construction materials, coupled with apparent insufficient supply of such materials by the TBBC. Monotonous food rations, largely dry food, creates a desire for fresh edibles, some of which can be grown inside the shelter, but others found outside. In addition, a mismatch seems to exist between the types of cooking fuel that are supplied by the TBBC and those favoured by the displaced people, resulting again in foraging for alternative cooking fuels. In addition, the shelters are not connected to regular water supply systems, meaning all water used must be collected from natural sources in and around the shelters.

Depletion of resources results in tension between the host communities and the shelter populations. Because bamboo, hardwoods and edibles are not always collected in sustainable ways, depletion of resources results, with secondary effects such as soil degradation and localised loss of biodiversity. Depletion of resources also creates new problems for the displaced people; such materials are likely to remain alive. The potential for competition and conflict is clear, and reduces the host communities' support for sustaining the temporary shelters in their areas. Real conflicts over scarce resources such as water have not been reported yet, but may arise in the future.

The waste problems concern both solid and liquid waste, from toilet, kitchen and bathroom use. The shelters partly lack adequate sanitary infrastructure and waste disposal services. Waste is a problem that is not only felt within the shelters, but also outside, especially in villages and settlements located downstream along the creeks and rivers running through the shelters.

Parts of the shelters lack adequate sanitation and drainage infrastructure. Latrines sometimes lacked septic tanks, and waste water from kitchen use is often allowed to run into the streets and off the slopes into the creeks at the shelters' base. Treatment of waste water is insufficient or non-existent, and natural water sources, both creeks and groundwater, get contaminated, the effects of which are also felt by the people living in villages downstream, who also depend on these water sources. Within the shelters, bad smells and health hazards abound. The RTG's policy to disallow the construction of durable sanitation and drainage infrastructure seems to be an important explanatory factor for this situation.

NGOs have put considerable effort into organising solid waste collection and disposal systems. These work to a considerable extent, but field observations revealed waste is still randomly dumped inside and near the shelters, and also the official dump sites sometimes lack proper measures to prevent contamination of ground and surface water. Some sites were not lined with plastic while others were found to be located dangerously close to natural water sources, with resulting unnecessary contamination of ground and surface water. Rotting garbage spread across the shelters causes bad smells and attracts vermin and other disease-carrying vectors. The practice of open space trash burning adds to the smell nuisance and carries the danger of producing unhealthy smoke when plastics, Styrofoam packaging, batteries and other hazardous materials are burned.

The solid waste problem not only stems from inadequate infrastructure; displaced peoples' behavior is also a factor. All shelters studied have a waste collection and disposal system, but random dumping of waste by the inhabitants still occurs. Interventions addressing the waste problem should focus on both infrastructure improvement and behavioural change.

Taken together, the liquid and solid waste problem in and around the shelters is high and seriously negatively affects the quality of both the environment and life for those inside and outside the shelters.

Key recommendations:

1. Allowing the use of durable construction materials, and/or provide more generous supplies of temporary construction materials collected in environmentally responsible ways
2. Diversify food rations or provide displaced persons with more opportunities to grow food by themselves. If necessary, educate people about high density food production such as pot gardening and sustainable agricultural practices. Consider the provision of additional land, not primary forest but already cultivated areas or areas with secondary growth instead
3. Provide greater encouragement to displaced people to use the cooking fuels supplied
4. Develop infrastructural solutions, temporary but effective and sustainable, for waste water management, with exact strategies determined at shelter level, depending on topography, shelter layout, available infrastructure and other conditions
5. Use three-pronged approach to solid waste management, seems to require a three-pronged approach consisting of infrastructural measures such as lining of landfills, management measures such as more frequent collection, and measures aimed at provoking behavioural change such as education or systems of punishment and reward. Detailed evaluations of the situation in each of the shelters will determine which combination of measures is most appropriate for each case
6. Explore using solid waste such as animal dung to generate energy in the shelters. Thailand already has the Small Power/Very Small Power Producer Programs (SPP/VSPP) with much knowledge and experience of small-scale power production using renewable resources including various types of waste. There is scope for transferring knowledge, granting loans and providing technical assistance
7. Consider connecting the shelters to the regular power grid, reducing the need for battery use and kerosene and making noisy generators redundant
8. Train and educate the shelter inhabitants to solve their environmental problems and issues, both educational activities aimed at changing environmentally unfriendly behavior, and vocational training programmes aimed at providing people with particular skills in construction, agriculture or other areas that will improve environmental conditions within the shelters and reduce their use of resources outside the shelters
9. Create awareness among those in command of the displaced people situation that sustainable or environmentally friendly solutions do not necessarily equate

to permanent solutions and that the benefits of such solutions will not only be felt within the shelters, but also beyond, and not only now, but also in the future. Also, that increasing the self-reliance the shelter populations is a way to reduce the burden on the RTG and other stakeholders.

Other more detailed recommendations can be found in the report.

Chapter 1
Introduction

Suwattana Thadaniti, Kanokphan U-Sha, Bart Lambregts, Jaturapat Bhiromkaew, Saowanee Wijitkosum, Vollop Prombang and Suchaow Toommakorn

Abstract The rationale for the study is outlined, briefly summarising the protracted nature of the displaced persons issue on the Thai–Myanmar border, the potential environmental impacts of the temporary shelters, notably the use of construction materials, the consumption of food and the production of various solid and water waste. Key research questions are posed, looking at actual impacts and consequences, and a variety of research techniques are used to analyse physical and behavioural impacts. Participative approaches are used to find out the views of both displaced persons and local communities who must share the resources.

Keywords Thai refugee policy · Displaced persons · Burmese refugees · Environmental impact · Research objectives · Research methodology

---

S. Thadaniti (✉)
Social Research Institute, Chulalongkorn University, Bangkok, Thailand
e-mail: tsuwattana@yahoo.com

K. U-Sha
Institute of Asian Studies, Chulalongkorn University, Bangkok, Thailand

B. Lambregts
Division of Urban and Environmental Planning, Faculty of Architecture,
Kasetsart University, Bangkok, Thailand

J. Bhiromkaew
Royal Thai Police, Bangkok, Thailand

S. Wijitkosum
Environmental Research Institute, Chulalongkorn University, Bangkok, Thailand

V. Prombang
Royal Thai survey department, Bangkok, Thailand

S. Toommakorn
Pisut Technology Consultant Company, Bangkok, Thailand

S. Thadaniti and S. Chantavanich (eds.), *The Impact of Displaced People's Temporary Shelters on Their Surrounding Environment*, SpringerBriefs in Environment, Security, Development and Peace 16, DOI: 10.1007/978-3-319-02842-2_1,

1.1 Statement of the Problem

The displaced person situation along the Thai–Myanmar border has lasted around 26 years, and has resulted in long-term settlement in various locations. The nine temporary shelter locations for the displaced people from Myanmar are situated along the Thai–Myanmar border, in five provinces in the Northern and Western regions of Thailand. The two regions have similar landforms and topography. For the two regions, natural morphology is characterised by high mountainous terrain and adequate water supply. The environs of the displaced persons' temporary shelters consist of abundant natural resources, biodiversity and healthy forests. Most temporary shelters are located in national forest reserves, which serve necessary food and shelter to the local communities (World Rainforest Movement 2002).

The temporary shelters may contribute to forest encroachment, exploitation and massive usage of natural resources and other environmental damages. Nowhere is this more critical than in relation to forestry. During humanitarian assistance provision, land can be partly or fully cleared to make way for the physical infrastructure of new shelters or settlements. Wood is commonly cut or gathered for cooking, heating and converting into charcoal. All of these activities to support life and livelihoods have potential to cause important environmental impacts on community or region.

If not appropriately addressed, the physical impacts of displaced people on the environment can be a long-term problem for displaced people, local residents and the host countries. The possible environmental impacts, in turn, provoke challenges for humanitarian agencies in the design of assistance programmes to displaced people. Research on the environmental impact of population from temporary shelters is needed as part of finding sustainable solutions or the well-being and health both the displaced people and local residents.

1.2 Research Objectives

1. To assess the environmental impacts of the population from the temporary shelters on the surrounding environment.
2. To identify and assess the negative impacts and optimise the positive elements of the environmental impacts of the temporary shelters for displaced people.

1.3 Research Questions

1. What is the current situation of the environment in and around the displaced people's temporary shelters?
2. What are the attitudes to the displaced people from local communities near the temporary shelters on sharing natural resources?

3. Are there any practices or behaviours linked to current environmental problems?
4. What are the impacts of displaced people's way of life on the environment, particularly on the use of forest, watershed, water sources and forest products and on nearby communities?

1.4 Study Framework

Provision of assistance by many agencies, including TBBC, UNHCR, other NGOs, donors and host and local government impacts on the environment, for example the provision of safe, clean drinking water, the physical location of the temporary shelters or settlements and provision of food assistance (Fig. 1.1).

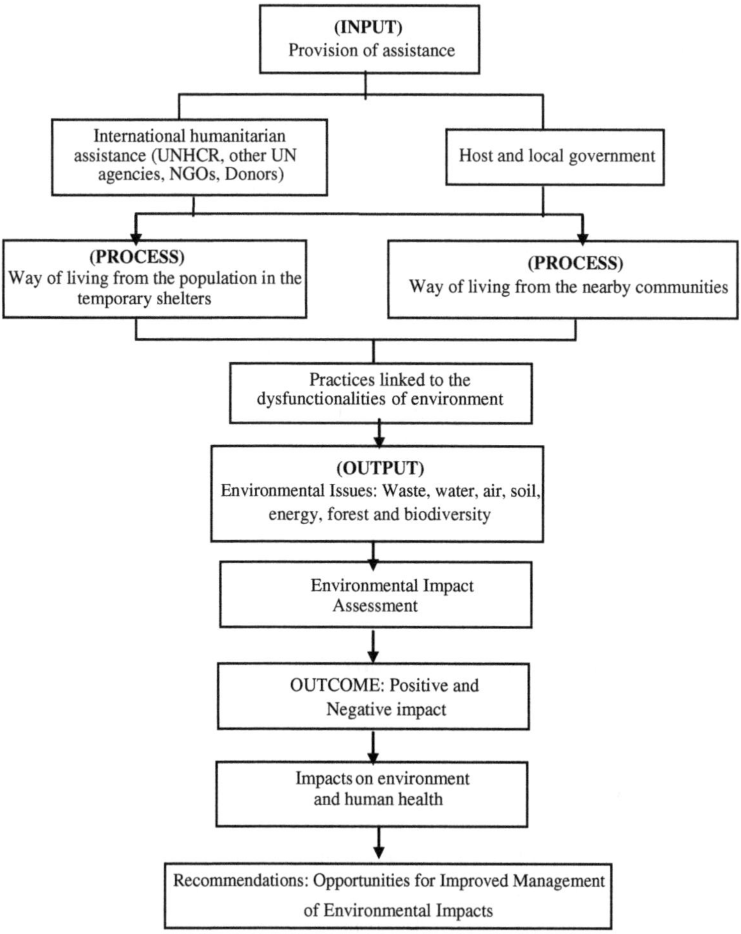

Fig. 1.1 Environmental input–output analysis chart. *Source* The authors

The assistance is regarded as the input to the displaced people who react for their survival and their quality of life. These inputs, therefore, are processed and generate the outputs that are factors or issues influencing the environment. These include waste, water, air, soil, climate, energy, forest and biodiversity. The environmental issues will be assessed to identify their impacts, and outcome of the assessment will be considered as positives and negatives based on the health and quality of life of the displaced people. After the environmental input–output analysis, recommendations will be made to mitigate and prevent the negative as well as to sustain the positive impacts for the future benefits, whether for displaced people or local communities.

1.5 Research Methodology and Analytical Tools

1.5.1 Method and Tools

Following the principles of Environmental Impact Assessment (EIA), the research techniques were both in social sciences and spatial sciences. Desk review examined documents and data related to the provision of assistance together with the displaced people's way of living to provide background of the environmental situation as the input and processing steps of the analysis. Participatory and non-participatory field surveys were conducted in the studied temporary shelters. The participatory surveys and observation included a questionnaire and in-depth interviews. Non-participatory surveys and maps, temporary shelter site analysis and gathering natural resource samples to study environmental qualities, for example, water and soil samples, have been used. The Geographical Information System (GIS) technique was used on particular components such as deforestation, flood, road rehabilitation and feature of interest to the environmental impacts.

1.5.2 Identification of Environment Quality

1.5.2.1 Quality Study of Natural Resources

Primary Study

The primary study analysed the impacts of the environmental quality in the study area on the surrounding environment by using on-site data collection, conducting field surveys, interview and observing the natural resources used and consumed by the displaced people, including water consumption behaviour, wastewater disposal and water drainage management, topography of the area, the locations of water resource, distance between temporary shelters to the water resources, study of the direction of the water flow and current water management system. The level of resources consumed by the displaced people was used to determine the amount of contaminated environs that is being generated each day.

In-Depth Study

Where the primary study indicated the level of environmental consumption in the temporary shelters was likely to have an impact on natural resources in nearby areas, an in-depth study was conducted to monitor the quality in natural resource nearby or where a negative impact will occur. Measurements of water quality included biochemical oxygen damage (BOD), dissolved oxygen (DO), acidity and water temperature and water colour index.

1.5.2.2 Solid Waste Study

The study obtained information on the amounts of waste disposed, waste characterisations, types, people behaviour on waste disposal, waste collection and disposal management by conducting a field survey, interview, observation and using a random sampling method in which waste was sampled from residential areas to determine the disposal rate per household per day and to analyse how waste is being managed in the study areas to verify the impact of solid waste and waste managing methods.

Reference

World Rainforest Movement, 2002: *Thailand: Displaced Peoples Wrongly Blamed for Forest Destruction*; at: http://www.wrm.org.uy/bulletin/56.html#Thailand.

Chapter 2
Desk Review

Suwattana Thadaniti, Kanokphan U-Sha, Bart Lambregts, Jaturapat Bhiromkaew, Saowanee Wijitkosum, Vollop Prombang and Suchaow Toommakorn

Abstract The assessment of the environmental impact of refugee and displaced persons' settlements is examined, including the use of environmental impact assessments. Examples from settlements around the world are compared and contrasted, looking at different types of settlement, including informal and state-imposed. Both positive and negative environmental impacts are discussed, and example given of where the presence of incoming populations has actually improved certain environmental factors. The focus then turns to studies of the settlements on the Myanmar–Thai border, assessing what environmental impact there has been, who caused it and how and what effects there have been on local populations.

Keywords Burmese refugees · Environmental impact assessment · Refugee settlements · Forest management · Local communities

S. Thadaniti (✉)
Social Research Institute, Chulalongkorn University, Bangkok, Thailand
e-mail: tsuwattana@yahoo.com

K. U-Sha
Institute of Asian Studies, Chulalongkorn University, Bangkok, Thailand

B. Lambregts
Division of Urban and Environmental Planning, Faculty of Architecture, Kasetsart University, Bangkok, Thailand

J. Bhiromkaew
Royal Thai Police, Bangkok, Thailand

S. Wijitkosum
Environmental Research Institute, Chulalongkorn University, Bangkok, Thailand

V. Prombang
Royal Thai survey department, Bangkok, Thailand

S. Toommakorn
Pisut Technology Consultant Company, Bangkok, Thailand

S. Thadaniti and S. Chantavanich (eds.), *The Impact of Displaced People's Temporary Shelters on Their Surrounding Environment*, SpringerBriefs in Environment, Security, Development and Peace 16, DOI: 10.1007/978-3-319-02842-2_2,

2.1 The Environmental Effects of Displaced People's Settlements

Little research has been carried out into the environmental impacts of the temporary shelters in Thailand. Environmental impact assessments (EIA) that have been carried out by NGOs, UNEP and other international organisations, or academics, have mostly focused on cases in Eastern Europe and Africa. However, these provide useful information on methods and tools used in EIAs of temporary shelter situations, with most studies suggesting linkage between temporary shelter locations and negative environmental impacts on the health and well-being of both the displaced people and the local communities.

Among the most significant problems associated with displaced people-affected areas are deforestation, soil erosion and depletion and pollution of water resources. Changes in the social and economic welfare of local communities following the arrival or during prolonged residency of displaced people can be significant, altering the rate of current and future local services available to people.

UNHCR is aware of the potential environmental impact of displaced people. Competition for natural resources such as fuelwood, building materials, fresh water and wild foods is an immediate concern. Evidence from several temporary shelters shows the importance of appropriate policies being implemented to control negative impacts. UNHCR reports that temporary shelters impact on natural resources such as soil and water, on the ecosystem, and on health and social issues such as competition for resources between local and displaced people and inadequate land use planning.

Examples of environmental concerns arise in different forms. Water problems emerge from the supply and management system as well as activities linked to it. Improper disposal of waste water could cause ground water contamination, soil erosion and floods. Deforestation due to construction, and use of energy resources for cooking and heating, could deteriorate soil quality and create flooding. Overcrowding and poor quality of shelters could produce undesired diseases and health problems for both local and displaced people.

Water pollution as one of the environmental impacts of displacement was reviewed by UNEP in the Sudan (UNEP 2007). Oversized concentrations of people in temporary dwellings raises concerns for sanitation and bacteriological contamination of surface and groundwater. The standard solution is the construction of pit latrines, though these are not in place everywhere. The most severe pollution problems were observed in temporary shelters in the more humid regions of Sudan. UNEP field teams found major water pollution issues surrounding all informal temporary shelters during their visit in Southern Sudan. Similar conditions of areas elsewhere were proved to be sources of epicentres for the cholera epidemic in 2006.

Different concerned parties have different perceptions on environmental degradation issues. Jacobsen (1997) defined *environmental impact* as the process of change that occurs with respect to forests, soil and water. Even where local people and displaced persons think their way of using the natural resources is sustainable;

there are often threats to particular ecosystems as viewed by national governments and international agencies. The environmental impacts of an influx of displaced persons can be large in the initial period as they enter and pass through the area with little regard to their impact compared to their security and survival. According to the analysis on 400,000 Rwandan displaced persons entered into the Ngara and Karagwe in the western Tanzania in April–June 1994, extensive damage on fields and crops resulted as they harvested foodstuffs on a particular border area where large groups of displaced persons stayed for several days, and demand for water use increased. The nature of environmental impacts then changes along when the emergency phase passes.

2.2 Type of Settlement

There are several forms of displaced person settlement. One way is for self-settlement in which displaced persons are unregistered and receive assistance for food, housing and land from local communities as loans or by paying rent. Alternatively, organised settlements can be established where they are registered and receive official assistance (Zetter 1995, as cited in Jacobsen 1997), such as the emergency relief shelters and reception centres set up by UNHCR and host country governments. However, these shelters can became permanent and remain populated for many years, as in the case of displaced persons from Cambodia in Thailand in 1979–1992 (Jacobsen 1997) and displaced persons from Myanmar on Thai–Myanmar border presently.

Agricultural settlement was developed by UNHCR and host governments in 1960s as an alternative to shelters. Agricultural settlement has multi-purposes, promoting displaced person self-sufficiency to reduce the burden of host governments, receiving communities and international communities for long-term financial responsibilities, avoiding the need to admit displaced persons for settlement in their territories and also promoting rural development (Daley 1993; Kibreab 1991; Lassailly-Jacob 1994; Zetter 1995, as cited in Jacobsen 1997).

2.3 Direct Environment Impact of Different Settlement Types

2.3.1 Organised Settlement

Relief agencies and host governments have argued that environmental damage with large groups of displaced persons is inevitable and thus the shelter settlement is better than spreading out in the region. The impact on the environment and local communities can be controlled when the displaced persons are segregated and sheltered because relief agencies can provide food, firewood and fuel alternatives and water, reducing extracting the resources from nearby environments and reducing the economic and cultural impact on the local communities (Jacobsen 1997).

However, there are several environmental problems relating to the shelter settlements. There will be partial deforestation in the initial influx in order to build shelters, provide construction materials and fuelwood. Also, the large number of residents in shelters means the need for fuelwood and food such as green vegetables cannot be met fully by relief agencies. The aid delivery can also be delayed by months especially because of transportation difficulty in the rainy season. Therefore, displaced persons inevitably seek out their needs from outside the shelters (Wilson et al. 1989; GTZ 1994, as cited in Jacobsen 1997). Additional problems occur when the displaced persons raise animals, although this is usually prohibited in the shelters; this impacts on the supply of firewood, grass and water inside the shelters, which all decline.

Agricultural settlement can also result in population expansion, with insufficient land and the restricted available geographical area. Host governments allocate the land and provide administrative services, and NGOs and UNHCR provide seeds, tools and other assistance (Lassailly-Jacob 1993, as cited in Jacobsen 1997). However, official land allocation is not always enough to meet the basic needs of displaced persons, and when they are also confined into the organised settlement without having met their needs, the continuous cultivation on soil without fallow periods can happen, as in African settlements, which results in soil degradation and thus decline in total production. This is one of the major problems in African settlements (Kibreab 1991, as cited in Jacobsen 1997). Furthermore, as the restriction on the allocated areas is imposed, the displaced persons cannot go far for grazing fuelwood which results in overusing the resources in the settled areas (Jacobsen 1997).

Environmental problems in the organised shelters also derive from the day-to-day operation of the shelters. In order to control disease-carrying vectors such as rats and mosquitoes, considerable amounts of insecticides and pesticides are used which can lead to toxic residues in the soil, water, humans and animals (Gurman 1991, as cited in Jacobsen 1997). Waste disposal such as packaging materials, human and medical waste and waste water can lead to pollution or become breeding sites for vectors if they are improperly disposed of (Jacobsen 1997).

Access to water is also a major problem. When displaced persons arrive in an emergency, water is an immediate need and little time can be given for the impact studies or design. As a result, wells may be dug without the assessment of the capacity of the aquifer that feeds them and thus lead to the rapid depletion rates or a decline in water quality (Hoerz 1995, as cited in Jacobsen 1997).

2.3.2 *Self-Settlement*

The environmental impact of self-settled displaced persons can be similar to the shelters and agricultural settlement. Though it is much more difficult to determine the impact, evidence suggests an increase in deforestation with land cleared to build dwellings and create agricultural land for displaced persons. Overgrazing can lead to loss of seedlings and browse trees (Jacobsen). The crucial difference between the self-settled displaced persons and organised shelter-based displaced persons is that the demand and pressure on local resources imposed by self-settled displaced persons is less concentrated and more widely distributed throughout the receiving region. In the case of Malawi, the effect on the demand of local fuelwood was less than the concentrated displaced persons in large shelters in the district of Dedza and Ntcheu (Wilson et al. 1980, as cited in Jacobsen 1997).

2.3.3 Indirect Environment Impact and Potential Conflicts with Host Communities

Conflict over natural resource use is derived from the indirect mechanisms of social, cultural and economic variables (Baechler 1999; Kahl 1998, as cited in Martin 2005). The competition to access to resources relies on the perception of inequality which results in hardening of group identities and then produces unfriendliness towards the outside groups. Whether or not this society-nature dynamic occurs depends on the intervening variables which determine if the conflicts over the use of resources will result in productive or unproductive pathways. Political economy of resource scarcity has intervening variables which also determine whether it leads to the competitive or cooperative actions (Martin 2005) (Table 2.1).

Jacobsen (1997) distinguished the relationship between the types of displaced persons settlement and the host communities over the use of environmental resources. He explained that different ways of organising of displaced persons can influence the relationship with local communities.

Table 2.1 Socioeconomic variables that frame social constructions of environmental scarcity

Category	Variables	Studies
Political	Leadership, formal and informal institutions and rules, including property and resource management systems	Schmidtz (2000)
Economic	Poverty and inequality	De Soysa/Gleditsch (1999)
	Economic interdependence	Neumayer (2002)
	Resource dependence	Martin/Lemon (2001)
Cultural	Family structures, religion, ethnicity	Baechler (1999)
Historical	Memories of economic change	Stewart (2002)
	Memories of local politics	Kurimoto (2002)
External intervention	Domestic and international development assistance	Suliman (1999)

Source Martin (2005)

Self-settled displaced persons have daily contact with the local people and they are obliged to live and work together and thus displaced persons extensively depend on the goodwill of the local host. For the shelter-based displaced persons, they can have access to official assistance and their relationship with the local communities is limited and they are less dependent on them. There can be local resentment about the benefits available for the displaced persons in the shelters. In the case study of Bonga, a displaced person shelter in western Ethiopia, the local community felt resentful towards displaced persons, complaining that the access to resources was more difficult than before the displaced persons arrived. Displaced persons stole their crops and water, and destroyed their irrigation channels, used illegal fishing methods and spoiled the traditional grazing land. The local people did not feel satisfied because there was a lack of benefits for them from shelter establishment. UNHCR promised several benefits at the beginning but these never materialised, which made the local communities perceive themselves as victims and displaced persons as the privileged groups (Martin 2005). Self-settled displaced persons, by the nature of their existence, have more local integration, whereas the shelter-based displaced persons have less pressure as they are less connected and less dependent on their local community host.

For displaced persons in agricultural settlement, they have more interaction with the local communities. In the case of Uganda (Hoerz 1996, as cited in Jacobsen 1997), informal interaction such as marriage, livestock and land negotiations existed among displaced persons and the local population.

The relationship with local communities plays a major role for the well-being of displaced persons and the environmental impacts, especially for self-settled displaced persons. The host communities are more influential in determining whether or how displaced persons can use and access communal land and local resources. The deeper consequences of the impact on environment livelihood is that not only do the displaced persons rely on the natural resources such as forest and forest products, grazing and water, but also the local population is relying on the same resources for their survival, which lead to rapid depletion. Moreover, the unsustainable way of using the infrastructure such as schools, roads and clinics can threaten the environmental livelihood of not only the displaced persons but also the local populations. In this context, the willingness of the local community to support and assist the displaced persons settlement is important. In the worse case situation, there can be a conflict over natural resources between the two populations (Black 1998).

In some cases, the local people share their knowledge on local ecology to displaced persons so that they are better educated on how to use the resources available efficiently (Jacobsen 1997). In addition, whether displaced persons will have access to land and common property resources such as fuelwood, grazing and water really depends on the goodwill of the local community, especially the community leaders. In South Africa's eastern Transvaal region, the refugees who knew the head of the community had better access to the resources than those who did not have connections (de Jongh 1994, as cited in Jacobsen 1997).

Jacobsen (1997) argued that large shelters and settlements both have their own negative impacts. Segregating displaced persons from the local community slows the development of land use practices which can be sustainable and compatible with the local practices. For self-settlement, displaced persons might finally be able to develop the mechanism for using and controlling the resources, but this process largely depends on the support and assistance from the local population. On the other hand, shelters are still probably needed for those who have less capacity for self-reliance such as the old and the infirm, orphaned children and single parents and sometimes during the time of drought when the displaced persons need to have food security and cannot provide themselves from outside the shelters (Kuhlman 1994, as cited in Jacobsen 1997). Neither the organised settlements nor self-settlement can guarantee the reduction in environmental degradation unless the community has good regulation mechanisms in place over the use of natural resources so that the displaced persons are incorporated into them.

The impacts on the environment from displaced persons should be seen as *a process that depends on many factors, and which can be mitigated with the involvement of all parties: displaced persons, local people, host governments and international assistance*. The solution to the environmental degradation is highly related to the local integration of displaced persons to the host community. The types of settlement are one of the important and influential factors to help the gradual integrating into the local community and thus likely to have environmental benefits (Jacobsen 1997).

2.4 Positive and Negative Environmental Impacts

Research by Oucho (2007) divided environmental impacts into negative and positive, based on a study of internally displaced people in forest land in West Africa;

2.4.1 Negative Impacts on Environment

- Decrease in tree and particular tree species (e.g. for timber and oil palm); causing soil erosion (by sun, wind and water) resulting in physical degradation of the top soil
- Disturbance of natural water resources and pollution
- Increase in health hazards
- Creation of waste due to dumping, mineral extraction and sand mining
- Decline in agricultural land and production, leading to food shortages and poor nutrition
- Decrease in the quantity of wood for building and energy

- Loss of biodiversity, especially natural medicines and traditional domestic products.

Dividing the earth's sphere into four areas, the impacts can be seen as follows:

- Biosphere, the flora and fauna: displaced people exerted impact on forestry and other vegetation which in turn impacted on local communities. Their engagement in deforestation was to meet their own survival needs, and to earn money
- Lithosphere, the land: most temporary shelters were overpopulated, resulting in rapid land degradation. Soil degradation took place and land usage rights arose as displaced people farmed the land without the rotation which locals had observed
- Hydrosphere, the water: poor sanitation infrastructure led to spread of epidemics. Relief shelters constructed with haste led to rapid depletion of water sources and decline of water quality or even diversion of river courses away from the villages
- Atmosphere: this is the area in need of more research. The controversial issue was the effect of increased carbon dioxide. However, the burning of forests resulted in the emission of gases that were harmful to human life. The absence of viable waste disposal facilities was a risk health hazard.

Other impacts ranged from poaching by displaced people led to loss of biodiversity. Arrival of displaced people impacted infrastructure and development resources as they help themselves to anything that would help them survive, including burning school desks, filling available latrines and overstretching the local health facilities.

2.4.2 Positive Impacts on Environment

- Transfer of swampland development and cultivation skill from displaced people to host populations
- Exchange of plantation management skills for perennial crops between displaced people and host populations
- Transfer of entrepreneurial skills from displaced people to host populations
- Increase in people's consciousness.

Intervention of donor agencies, host governments and the displaced people themselves invariably impacted positively in the environment, economic, social and political aspects of the local community. For example, the displaced people or IDPs provided cheap labour for the villages. Their presence created economic opportunities.

EIAs of displaced people indicate both negative and positive impacts on the environment. With the intervention of humanitarian agencies, some studies suggested that negative impacts were eventually converted into positives, and consequently could, in turn, benefit the host communities.

2.5 Perceptions of International Agencies and Host Governments of the Environmental Impacts by Displaced People

The most visible and tangible evidence of the presence of displaced persons is the loss of vegetation cover because wood is needed for cooking and shelter. This abrupt change does not only impact environmentally but also socially and economically. The environmental impact of displaced persons is the concern for the host governments as well as the international community, including the aid agencies and the donor governments. The first practical reason is that displaced people are forced to rely on the natural resources for their survival in the initial short run.

Relief agencies provide for most immediate needs, but the unsustainable use of resources is a major concern because this can adversely effect the livelihoods of displaced persons themselves, especially if they live in exile for a long period. Sometimes, in the worst case, malnutrition, disease and increased poverty result (Black 1998).

The immediate impact on environmental livelihood is not the only reason of concern about displaced person settlements. There is also concern for the loss of biodiversity. At the 1993 Convention on Biological Diversity, it was agreed to elaborate more management plans and conservation agreements to protect the areas of special importance, such as forests, wetlands and diverse and rare species of flora and fauna. In this context, the immediate impact on the environmental livelihood from the influx of displaced persons is seen as a threat to the sustainability and longer term global concern to protect the endangered species (Black 1998).

It is evident that many governments are unwilling to accept displaced persons on stated grounds of environmental degradation. The governments of Honduras, Turkey and Tanzania stated that, because of the environmental issues, they were justified in closing their borders. However, it is politically convenient for governments to blame displaced persons for the cost of environment degradation, because they can justify strict control of asylum seekers or reject unwanted displaced persons. The burden of supporting displaced persons falls disproportionately on developing countries, and there are calls for richer countries to address the imbalance in offering asylum (Black 1998).

While admitting a temporary attitude towards resource management on the part of displaced persons might limit strategies that would promote sustainability, Kibreab (1997) has argued that such an attitude is more characteristic of governments and assistance agencies, rather than of displaced persons themselves (Kibreab 1997, as cited in Black 1998). Regarding poverty with relation to environmental degradation, Kibreab (1997) concluded from his own survey in eastern Sudan that the real reason for the environmental degradation was mechanised commercial rain-red crop production, clearing of vegetation for tractorisation, commercial firewood and charcoal production for cities. He continued that theoretically poverty actually drives motivation for more sustainable ways of using the natural resources because misusing the resources can bring bad consequences for the displaced persons' survival (Black 1998). Regarding the incentives for displaced persons to conserve the land, there was a link between lack of land tenure security and willingness to conserve the land.

But it is not only the displaced persons who are lack of land tenure security. In many parts of Africa, the introduction of new laws on the ownership of the land and nationalisation of common property resources has led to land grabs by rich people and open access to common property resources without effective control over the use (Black 1998).

Environmental degradation or conflicts between displaced people and local resident populations may, if not addressed, undermine the effectiveness of UNHCR's programmes and, equally importantly, influence the future decision of governments to offer asylum to displaced people. However, displaced people cannot be expected to put environmental considerations ahead of their own safety and welfare. This is where UNHCR and other organisations can provide assistance, by minimising environmental impacts and assisting host countries with rehabilitation and clean-up operations (UNHCR 2001).

Oucho (2007) has suggested that strategies for assisting displaced persons should coordinate of all parties involved. Eight lessons for the donor agencies to be considered are:

- environmental screening for development to take place
- relief agencies to become increasingly subject to environmental review
- proper understanding of the food basket items, which affect fuel requirements and resource use
- stronger inter-agency coordination during relief and recovery
- technical expertise to help avoiding environmental threats
- World Food Programme country offices to have guidance on the use and chemical disposal
- recycling and green procurement procedures throughout the World Food Programme.

2.6 Displaced People's and Local Communities' Participation in Environmental Management

Conserving natural resources mainly depends on the participation from displaced persons and local community in the same areas. Community-based natural resource management (CBNRM) approaches originated from the observation that local communities *frequently have more knowledge of local situations and thus better (or at least complementary) technical expertise than outside 'experts', as well as on the political principle that the interventions of external actors and agencies should be accountable to beneficiary populations as stakeholders* (Black 1998).

The principles of CBNRM are ownership of the resource and the project by stakeholders; organisation, such as a community-based structure to manage the project and resolve disputes; economic incentives so that the CBNRM approach remains in the economic interest of the communities and motivation and interest are high (Black 1998). Black suggested this approach be used with displaced persons although it is very difficult to generalise the context of overall displaced person situations. He gave the example of SHELTERFIRE project carried out in Zimbabwe, where the community participated in the decision-making processes; the management of wildlife brought mutual benefits rather than conflicts for both local communities and authorities and preserved the wildlife population better. A decline in poaching, an increasing elephant population and real cooperation for the natural resources management were the outcomes of including communities interest in the way resources were managed.

However, there are several difficulties from applying lessons from the specific success from the SHELTERFIRE project. There was already the market to generate revenues from for hunters to pay to shoot wild animals in a sustainable and controlled way. It is unlikely that in the context of displaced persons stable revenues could be earned in a situation where armed conflict had already uprooted mass populations. Nevertheless, commercialisation of forest products has potential for wealth generation, and possibly displaced persons can be involved (Black 1998).

Black gave one example of Joint Forest Management (JFM) project in India and Nepal (Nhira/Matose 1995, as cited in Black 1998) in non-displaced person situation. In this context, the protection of forest is partnership-based management between the local communities and logging companies (Myers 1991, as cited in Black 1998). He pointed out that commercialising the forest products is inevitable, and necessary to meet the demand for the population for economic improvement. Therefore, protecting the forests under controlled and managed logging rather than prohibiting it has become an important approach for international environmental organisations such as the World Wide Fund for Nature (WWF) and the International Union for the Conservation of Nature (IUCN) (Black 1998).

If the principle of economic incentive to conserve the environment is accepted, the question is whether the displaced persons or the situation of displaced persons can apply the two key principles from the CBNRM approach, ownership and organisation capacity of displaced persons at the community level. Access to land or other natural resources for the displaced persons is unusual especially in developing countries and thus might prevent participation in managing natural resources which they cannot own. But not only the displaced persons but also most of the rural population lack ownership and control over the land as most rural land is nationalised or owned by wealthy elites or international companies from the colonial era. In such circumstances, the CBNRM approach not only helps the managing of natural resources but also re-establishes the right of secure access to and control over land and natural resources and there is no technical reason why the displaced persons cannot participate in this process together with the local communities. On the other hand, there is an argument against this inclusion, that displaced persons have a fixed time for their stay, and thus lack of long-term participation for the sustainability of natural resources. Black asserted that both local communities and displaced persons are faced with challenges to balance out between the short and long-term interest and both have immediate incentives to maximise their income and both may have longer involvement. The only issue is the attitude of host communities and host governments for such involvement from the displaced persons in community-based approach to manage the natural resources (Black 1998).

For host communities, the exclusion of displaced persons in this process may bring some advantages to the access to land and other natural resources. However, displaced persons can benefit the local population by sharing their important skills and experience. For example, in southern Sudan, Ugandan displaced persons shared their agricultural techniques with the local people in a way which advanced the techniques of Sudanese hosts (Harrell-Bond 1986, as cited in Black 1998). The consequences of excluding the displaced persons might be that host communities may confront daily thefts of resources and potential social conflicts (Black 1998).

The attitude of host governments poses a difficulties for the international agencies which want to promote CBNRM approaches, who prefer not to see displaced persons as the direct beneficiaries of such policies. Black stated that the call for the link of humanitarian aid to the development programmes should be considered to provide the longer benefits to the host governments and their population (Black 1998).

2.7 Environment Impacts of Displaced People's Settlements Along the Thai-Myanmar Border

There are several criticisms about displaced persons causing environmental degradation and limiting the development of nearby hosting communities. However, there are not yet extensive studies about the impact on the environment from the displaced persons' lifestyle. Three studies have been conducted on the environmental impact of the Myanmar displaced person population in the shelters, with one focusing particularly on the practices of displaced persons in natural resource management, the causes of environmental degradation around both inside and around the shelters and the political and social consequences of environmental degradation.

2.7.1 *Contextual Changes Affecting Access to Land and Forest by Displaced People from Myanmar in Thailand*

Before 1990, the conditions for land tenure and access to the forest products were initially established by Thai villagers, landowners and local authorities from Ministry of Interior. In general, the forest areas for the displaced persons were defined by local villagers for collecting wood, bamboo and leaves to build houses, firewood or charcoal for fuel and bamboo shoots or roots for food. Some displaced persons still did gardening around their houses or cultivating crops on the Myanmar border side. There was small population spread over about 30 camps along the border area. The assistance from NGOs was at a minimum while having a high level of self-sufficiency (Gallasch 2001).

This context changed when the Myanmar military escalated its offensives in the mid 1990s, leading to shelters being consolidated for security issues, and more restrictions imposed upon the displaced persons staying in the shelters. Consequently, the Royal Forestry Department (RFD) put more restrictions on displaced persons' access to land tenure and forest products, and the dependency on the assistance from NGOs was increased.

2.7.2 *Access to the Forest Land and Products*

Nai Soi and Mae La shelters are located in the Economic and Agricultural Zones of Forest Reserves. The use of land tenure was facilitated by commercial landowners with concessions or land use certificates from RFD. In 1972, the areas around Nai Soi were declared a Forest Reserve. The Nai Soi shelter is situated on the land owned by a businesswoman who used to import teak, livestock and gems from KarenniState. She demanded 5,000 baht per month for compensation on the tenancy, and so the displaced persons sold their empty rice sacks to pay for the rental fees. Landownership rights have not been granted to anyone and the land tenure is recognised commonly with the Sitthi Tham Kin[1] certificate from RFD.

In Mae La shelter, local authorities from MOI confirmed that 70 % of the land where the shelter is located is owned by two businessmen from Maesot. At the time of the research, the businessmen claimed 300 million baht for losing their revenue as the land was earmarked for a joint business plan for cotton planting at Mae La with some Karen investors. However, no settlement has been reached yet

[1] Sitthi Tham Kin means RFD certificate recognising land use rights in Economic and Agricultural Zones of Forest Reserves. The research also stated that most of the villagers in the area also have Sor Kor 1 (Restricted land tenure certificate issued by Department of Land in Thailand) and Sor Por Kor (Land tenure certificate issued by Agricultural Land Reform Office after Forest Reserve are declassified by RFD).

at the time of the research conducted by Gallasch in 2001. Similarly, in Chaing Mai Tambon "X", the commercial landowners allow Shan displaced persons to stay on their land in exchange for cheap labour. In the Protected Areas of Mae Kong Kha and Nupho, MOI-assisted displaced persons to access land but RFD put more pressure on the relocation of those shelters. Accordingly, there is no land right by customary landowners in the Protected Areas but recognised and paid partly by displaced persons and relief NGOs (Gallasch 2001).

Environmental degradation is a serious issue (UNHCR/ILO 2007a) in and around the temporary shelters in Tak province. The natural resources such as bamboo and fuelwood around the shelters were taken by displaced persons because of shortage of housing materials as the family size increases and the policy from MOI not to build permanent structures, which in turn cause continuous housing repairs (UNHCR/ILO 2007a).

In Mae Hong Son, more pressure is imposed upon the access to natural resources because more population depends on forest cultivation. The establishment of shelters, the National Park, forest reserve and the wildlife sanctuary are the accumulated factors which limit the access to cultivated areas, as well as to forest products for the hosting communities (UNHCR/ILO 2007a).

2.7.3 Natural Resource Management in Displaced People Communities

Displaced person-related forest degradation has been significant where shelters were consolidated from 30 to 10 which led to high-density population and where Shan displaced persons were not protected. Villagers separated a specific area for displaced persons to collect forest products in order to prevent competition and protect over-exploitation. The research found that since displaced persons are indigenous people who came from similar forests, they respected the customary forest management of local villagers and regulated their collection of biological resources in a sustainable way.

In Nai Soi and Nupho shelters, NGOs supplied vegetable seeds and fruit tree seedlings to promote home gardening. The government authorities have also agreed that home gardening is a suitable way for food supplementary and soil erosion prevention. The research found that 5 % of displaced persons used organic compost for soil nutrition without using chemical fertilisers. However, in Mae La area, the home gardening is limited owing to high-density housing, which in turn has led to water shortages and lack of necessary seeds.

Regarding the water supply, displaced persons and villagers used water from different sources. Wastewater is managed mainly by building soak pits, and NGOs monitor the water quality downstream to minimise the pollution for local villagers. In spite of these measures, displaced persons in Mae La shelter and villagers downstream have suffered water depletion because of shelter consolidation. For

Shan displaced persons who depend on irrigation water, the Thai government does not allow NGOs to manage their water supplies and waste. The research asserted that water shortage was significant only where shelters were consolidated. The report done by UNHCR/ILO shows that at the shelters in Mae Hong Son province water supply in four shelters and the host communities are supplied by the catchment areas in higher areas. Domestic water for four shelters is sufficient for the whole year except in some areas where water is released at specific times in the dry season. The report shows that communities in Ban Nai Soi and Ban Mae Tor La do not have difficulty in obtaining water during the dry season. A survey, however, is needed for the other nine host communities.

Soil and river bank erosion are the problems for Ban Mai Surin (BMS) and Mae Ra Ma Luang (MRM). COERR has installed gabion boxes on a portion of river bank to prevent soil erosion in BMS. About 1,000 pineapple seedlings were given to new arrivals to plant for controlling soil erosion and were used as food source in MRM. In addition, in Mae La Oon (MLO), COERR has implemented road construction to control soil erosion integrated grass planting along the road side (UNHCR/ILO 2007a).

The report indicates that burning fields for planting occurred from March to April each year and the forest areas are also burned for growing edible mushrooms for local consumption and for new grass to attract animals which they hunt. Consequently, heavy air pollution occurs and affects the health of people living in the nearby areas. Local villagers along both the Thai and Myanmar borders, in addition, clear their planted areas by burning off fields (UNHCR/ILO 2007a).

The practices of disposing material wastes are the same for displaced persons inside and outside of shelters. Most displaced persons burned their rubbish, some reused for land refill, and a few recycled food rubbish to organic compost. NGOs in shelters constructed latrine pits for human excrement and monitored the pits to protect groundwater resources (Gallasch 2001).

2.7.4 Causes of Environmental Degradation in Forests that are Home to Displaced People

Gallasch (2001) asserted that the shelter population is not the major cause for forest degradation, but rather commercial agricultural, and forestry production. The subsistence agricultural practices by local villagers were restricted by RFD and it adversely affected the land degradation. Chemical spraying in commercial agricultural was merely regulated near Forest Reserves and it polluted irrigation canals and ground water resources near Tambon "X". Therefore, the unregulated chemical spraying and increase in restriction for local villagers to their subsistence agriculture and areas where Shan displaced persons were unprotected were the causes for environmental degradation. Regarding forest logging by displaced persons, Thai businesses with sawmills in Myanmar were the main cause of illegal logging. Only 2 % of displaced persons were hired by Thai for logging. Their involvement in forest logging was considered as an amateur operation with low wages and no safety protection (Gallasch 2001).

The decrease in agricultural land was caused by RFD policy on intensifying the cultivation which shortened the time for shrubs and grasses to regenerate the soil nutrition, leading in urn to soil erosion. Displaced persons are not, therefore, the cause of land degradation, but the restriction on customary land use and rotational cultivation by RFD. For soil nutrition, the population in the shelters in Mae La, Mae Kong Kha, has tripled from the shelters consolidation. Since then, Mae La and two Thai villages have faced water shortages. In addition, high-density housing in shelters reduced second vegetation and thus led to nutrition depletion in soil. The policy on shelter consolidation increases more population in the shelter and put more pressures on water and soil resources (Gallasch 2001).

2.8 Environmental Impacts of Displaced People's Temporary Shelters on Local Communities

The U.S. Committee for Refugees and Immigrants and ABAC Research Institute conducted a survey research on perceptions and attitudes of Thai people towards displaced people who sought asylum in Thailand. The survey was conducted in 11 provinces, four with shelters, seven without, between 28 April and 8 May 2007. Out of 2,900 respondents, the findings mostly showed negative perceptions and attitudes cited in Boonyaratana (2007):

- 73.1 % believed that displaced people could bring epidemics into the country
- 75.9 % believed that displaced people could bring chaos and danger into the country if the Thai government allowed them to work outside the shelter
- 71.1 % believed that displaced people were Thailand's burden
- 69.4 % believed that displaced people were a threat to the national security
- 64.2 % believed that displaced people might reduce the share of local employment
- 59.9 % believed that displaced people had a good living condition due to UN and other agencies' assistance.

Bandan/Thaweesak (2009) looked at attitudes of local people living in Mae La sub-district towards displaced people, with sample size 498; 57.2 % of the respondents felt indifferent about displaced people, while 33.5 % believed that such displaced people brought many problems, and 72.5 % believed that locating displaced people in the area would have negative impacts on themselves and the communities surrounding; 27.5 % believed there were benefits to local communities in terms of availably inexpensive employment and increase in trading activities. For other aspects, it was found that displaced people decreased security level by 32.9 %, health by 33.9 %, wildlife and natural resources by 96.8 % and environmental quality by 90.0 %, respectively. For living condition, 30.7 % of respondents reported that it was more difficult to earn the living. Out of 498,

62.7 % of the respondents believed that such impacts were the results of temporary shelters, while 37.3 % were the results of other factors.

According to the study, the most prominent problem is human trafficking, followed by deforestation, illegal immigrant, drugs and terrorism. The finding showed that such problems were most likely caused by the displaced people around the areas (33.5 %), followed by officials (25.4 %), local people (15.8 %), locally influential persons (13.0 %) and ineffective degrees of penalty (12.4 %).

In sum, the establishment of a temporary shelter in Mae La sub-district could result in various impacts, in terms of ways of living, quality of life and natural resources. Such effects have both negative and positive. However, it is likely that most impacts are negative, leading to concerns on environmental issues.

Tipaporn (2010) stressed that displaced peoples' temporary shelters might have caused problems to local communities. In terms of waste management, garbage generated from the temporary shelters was about 3.9 tonnes per day. For only Mae La sub-district in Tak province, there was about 2,539 tonnes of garbage dumped in 2008. The dump site is located next to Mae La village which, in turn, affected the quality of water in the creek as well as created air pollution around the areas (Kiriya 2009). Papers, plastic bags, cans and bottles slipped into the creek were clearly seen at the bottom of the creek during the drought season. The waste management problem around this area called for Catholic Office for Emergency Relief and Refugees (COERR) attention, and it has worked hard to educate the communities how to manage and reuse disposals since 2002. Due to budget shortage, however, this assistance has been brought to an end.

Natural resources in the community have been destroyed due to higher consumer demand from both from population in the communities and in the shelters. In addition to the local population, the status of around 10,000 of displaced people was not recognised by the state and private agencies, resulting in insufficient resource allocations. The displaced people had to struggle by themselves to earn a living. Some were victims of human trafficking. Some left the shelter, trespassing the national forest boundary to cut down trees. Deforestation is a key problem, exemplified by a seizure of about 300 of logs in Thailand (Bangkokbiznews 2009). Full-size trees had been cut, shipped across the river for processing in Myanmar and then shipped back to Thailand. For displaced people, the highest demand for wood is for housing.

As the number of displaced persons increases, competition for natural resource tends to be higher. People in the temporary shelters compete with the local people from communities nearby for varieties of plants such as bamboo, mushroom and other vegetables. As a result, there is a negative feedback from local people living in the communities nearby. Local people felt private organisations provide assistance and contributions to the displaced people, but not to the local communities. Instead of exploiting agricultural products from the local communities, these organisations brought food and products from outside entrepreneurs, meaning local products became less competitive at the lower price. Moreover, property crimes around the area increase as the stream of displaced people grow. Agricultural tools and products from local communities sometimes have been reported missing.

Nevertheless, local people living in the communities nearby reported some benefits to which the displaced people contribute. Labour cost is relatively inexpensive, some local products can be sold in the shelters, and local people can buy inexpensive products from displaced people living in the shelters.

In summary, based on the study of six villages around Mae La sub-district and Tha Song Yang district in Tak province, displaced persons' temporary settlements have generated problems to local communities, such as competition for natural resources, deforestation and pollutions, as well as other economic and social problems. According to the local administration of Mae La (2005), it was reported that enormous amounts of natural resources, for example bamboo, woods and vegetables had been exploited for people in the shelters, which in turn affect local Thai people's the way of life.

The local administration of Mae La alone cannot solve these problems. Local governments at a higher level or the Thai government itself are accountable for dealing with these problems, which have been affecting people in Mae La for more than 20 years. Local governments have to work in accordance with the RTG in restoring forest and fresh water, managing waste and sustaining natural resources. For human development, all agencies should provide basic needs, medical and occupational assistance.

References

Bangkok Biz News, 2009: *Thailand Border Survey on World Refugee Day,* (Bangkok: Bangkok Biz News).

Black, R., 1998: *Refugees, Environment and Development,* (London: Addison Wesley and Longman Ltd).

Gallasch, D., 2001: *Taking shelter under trees,* (Chiang Mai: Friends without Borders).

Jacobsen, K., 1997: "Refugees' Environmental Impact: The Effect of Patterns of Settlement", in: *Journal of Refugee Studies*, 10,1: 19–36.

Kibreab, G., 1997: "Environmental Causes and Impact of Refugee Movements: A Critique of the Current Debate", in: *Disasters*, 21,1: 20–38.

Martin, Adrian, 2005: "Environmental Conflict Between Refugee and Host Communities", in: *Journal of Peace Research,* 42,3: 329–346.

Mae La Local Administration Organisation, 2005: "Report on Displaced Persons Fleeing Fighting Problem Solving and the Impact on Mae La area", Mae La Local Administration Organisation (Unpublished document).

Mitchin, Keeriya, 2009: "A Border Story", in: *Friends Without Border*, 6,31.

Oucho, J. O., 2007: "Environmental Impact of Refugees and Internally Displaced Persons in Sub–Saharan Africa", Keynote Address to the African Migration Alliance Biennial Workshop on Climate Change, Environment and Migration, East London, South Africa, 15–16 November 2007.

UNEP, 2007: *Sudan post–conflict environmental assessment* (Nairobi: UNEP).

UNHCR, 2001: *Refugees and the Environment*; at: http://www.unhcr.org/3b039f3c4.html.

UNHCR/ILO, 2007a: *Livelihoods report: Volume 1, Tak Province* (Bangkok: UNHCR/ILO).

UNHCR/ILO, 2007b: *Livelihood report: Volume 1, Mong Hong Son Province* (Bangkok: UNHCR/ILO).

Chapter 3
Displaced Persons' Temporary Settlement Along the Thai–Myanmar Border: State of Affairs from an Environmental Perspective

Suwattana Thadaniti, Kanokphan U-Sha, Bart Lambregts, Jaturapat Bhiromkaew, Saowanee Wijitkosum, Vollop Prombang and Suchaow Toommakorn

Abstract The history of the displaced person's issue in Thailand is briefly summarised, including how many have settled and why. The three shelters studied are then described in environmental terms, including their locations, topography, natural disasters, climate, flora and fauna. The relationship of the local population to its environment, is described, including the sustainable use of natural resources. The changes caused by a large influx of displaced persons and their settlements are described.

Keywords Thai refugee policy · Environmental destruction · Settlement population · Forest management · Flora and fauna · Settlement location · Settlement topography

---

S. Thadaniti (✉)
Social Research Institute, Chulalongkorn University, Bangkok, Thailand
e-mail: tsuwattana@yahoo.com

K. U-Sha
Institute of Asian Studies, Chulalongkorn University, Bangkok, Thailand

B. Lambregts
Division of Urban and Environmental Planning, Faculty of Architecture, Kasetsart University, Bangkok, Thailand

J. Bhiromkaew
Royal Thai Police, Bangkok, Thailand

S. Wijitkosum
Environmental Research Institute, Chulalongkorn University, Bangkok, Thailand

V. Prombang
Royal Thai survey department, Bangkok, Thailand

S. Toommakorn
Pisut Technology Consultant Company, Bangkok, Thailand

S. Thadaniti and S. Chantavanich (eds.), *The Impact of Displaced People's Temporary Shelters on Their Surrounding Environment*, SpringerBriefs in Environment, Security, Development and Peace 16, DOI: 10.1007/978-3-319-02842-2_3,

3.1 Displaced People Along the Thai–Myanmar Border: Background Characteristics

3.1.1 History

Although Thailand is not a party to the 1951 Refugee Convention or the 1967 Protocol, the Royal Thai Government (RTG) has hosted refugees from neighbouring countries since 1965 (Prungchit Phanawathanawong 2007). Myanmar refugees have found shelter in Thailand since 1984 when fights broke out between the Karen National Union (KNU) and Myanmar's armed forces. The armed conflict initially caused around 6,000 Karen to flee into Thailand. These people were received along the Thai–Myanmar borders, and given emergency assistance by the Ministry of Interior (MOI) and NGOs that had been working with Indochinese refugees in Thailand before. The first refugee camp to be created was Huay Kaloke, located at Amphoe Mae Sot in the province of Tak. As the fighting went on, people continued to flee into Thailand. The year 1995 saw an especially dramatic increase, triggered by the falling apart of the KNU. More temporary settlements were built to receive these refugees. At that time, temporary settlements built by the Thai Government came in various types. Some of them were called *concentration camps* or *displaced persons camps* until the Thai Government declared all camps to be officially named *temporary shelters* and the refugees themselves *displaced person fleeing from fighting*, this to avoid the use of the words *refugee camp* and *refugee*. The latter was considered undesirable because the Thai Government had not signed the Convention related to the Status of Refugees with the UNHCR, and because the MOI viewed the Myanmar newcomers as having illegally entered the country.

As a result of this, the displaced people are considered to be subject to the Thai Immigration Act of BE 2522 of 1979. So far there have not been any cabinet resolutions to endorse the displaced people's temporary stay in Thailand as is required by Article 17 of the Act, only a Resolution of the National Security Council with executive discretion. Displaced people who leave the camps are subjected to arrest, and they may be charged for illegal entry (Pornpimol Trichot 2005). However, simultaneously Thailand will facilitate and assist the temporary shelters on the basis of humanitarian principles and with regard for the principle of non-refoulement. Displaced persons will not be forced to involuntary move back to their country or put in danger (Jirasak Masantiar 2000).

3.1.2 Demography of the Displaced People

The demography of displaced people in shelters tends to fluctuate with the intensity of fighting in Myanmar between the ethnic minorities and the SPDC.[1] While *veterans* sometimes leave for resettlement, new arrivals add to the numbers. The total TBBC verified caseload in 2010 included registered displaced persons and unregistered people. The UNHCR registered population was 101,358. UNHCR figures generally do not acknowledge new entries since 2005 although they include 243 persons presented for PAB consideration and 3,069 students who reside in the temporary shelters for education purposes. The TBBC figure also includes 653 displaced persons in Wieng Heng who are not included in the UNHCR caseload (TBBC 2010) (Fig. 3.1).

In 2005, the RTG allowed a third countries resettlement programme to take off after it realised that deportation to Myanmar would not be a viable option for the near future due to the prolonged political conflicts in Myanmar. Altogether 6,111 displaced persons left Thailand for resettlement in the first half of 2010, bringing the total since 2006 to 595,171. Total resettlement numbers in 2010 are expected to be around 10,000 and similar numbers are anticipated for 2011 (TBBC 2010).

Currently, there are nine temporary shelters located in four provinces of Thailand. They are Ban Mai Nai Soi, Ban Mae Surin and Mae La Oon in Mae Hong son Province, Mae La, Umpiem Mai and Nu Po in Tak Province, Don Yang in Kanchanaburi Province and Tham Hin in Ratchaburi Province. The RTG is in charge of the management of these temporary shelters. The authorised ministry is the MOI. It takes care of the governance of the temporary shelters in collaboration with the temporary shelter committees. The temporary shelter committees are elected for 2-year periods and focus on a variety of issues regarding the displaced persons including education, health, food distribution, sexual and gender-based violence (SGBV), judiciary issues, women's issues, security and youth issues. For the seven Karen Temporary Shelters, the committees have to report to the Karen Refugee Committee (KRC) and to the Karenni Refugee Committee (KNRC) for Karenni Temporary Shelters. The committees have the responsibility for the overall administration of the temporary shelters and for communications with the Thai authorities, donors and NGOs (DFID 2008).

The RTG's policy on displaced persons is implemented through provincial and district authorities. These manage the daily life in temporary shelters by cooperating with the temporary shelter committees and displaced persons. Other agencies such as the MOI volunteers and the Border Patrol Police are also engaged in policy implementation, as well as in the provision of security and surveillance of the displaced persons. A local district officer usually acts as the shelter commander for a temporary shelter. Nightly safety and curfews are managed by displaced person staff in collaboration with Thai paramilitaries (Vogler 2007).

[1] State Peace and Development Council: the official name of the ruling military junta in Myanmar, successor to the previous "State Law and Order Restoration Council" assumed after the shakeup of 1990.

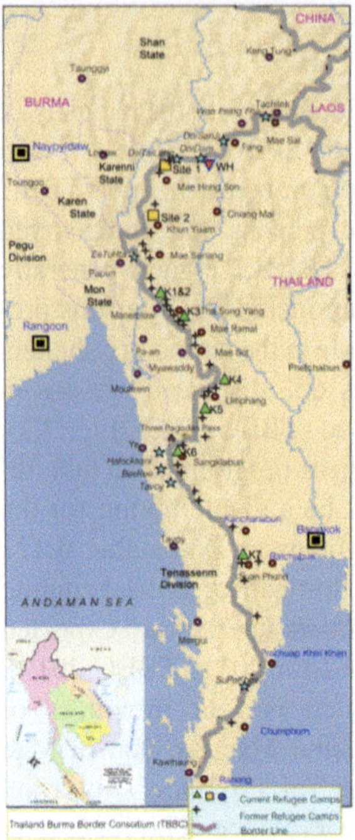

	TBBC Verified Caseload[1] 31 Jul-10	UNHCR Population[2] 31 Jul-10 Female	Male	Total
Cheingmai Province				
WH Wieng Heng (Shan Refugees)	**653**			
Mae Hong Son Province				
Site 1 Ban Kwai/Nai Soi[3]	**15,341**	6,477	6,622	13,099
Site 2 Ban MaeSurin	**3,574**	1,144	1,192	2,336
K1 Mae La Oon (Site3)	**16,070**	6,282	6,713	12,995
K2 Mae Ra Ma Luang (Site 4)	**18,536**	6,231	6,360	12,591
Subtotal:	**53,251**	20,134	20,887	**41,021**
Tak Province				
K3Mae La	**46,329**	15,363	15,177	30,540
K4 Umpiem Mai	**17,476**	6,131	6,302	12,433
K5 Nu Po	**15,282**	4,888	5,041	9,929
Subtotal:	**79,150**	26,382	26,520	**52,902**
Kanchanaburi Province				
K6 Ban Don Yang	**4,528**	1,517	1,489	**3,060**
Ratchaburi Province				
K7 Tham Hin	**8,711**	2,252	2,123	4,375
Subtotal:	**146,563**	50,339	51,019	**101,385**

IDP camps	
Wan Peing Fha	**2,981**
Doi San Ju	**395**
Doi Dam	**252**
Doi Tai Lang	**2,371**
Ee Tu Hta	**4,596**
Halochanee	**3,279**
Bee Ree	**3,331**
Tavoy	**2,340**
Total	**19,545**

State of Origin of UNHCR pop.

- 61% **Karen**
- 17% **Karenni**
- 7% **Tenasserim**
- 5% **Mon**
- 6% **Pegu**
- 1% **Irrawaddy**
- 1% **Rongoon**
- 2% **Other**

☆ IDP Site

▽ Wieng Heng: Camp Committee

□ Site1 & 2 ; Karenni Refugee Committee (KnRc)

△ Camp K1-K7: Karen Refugee Committee (KnRc)

Notes:

1. The TBBC verified caseload includes all persons verified as living in the camps and eligible for rations, registered or not (including students) except new arrivals in Mae La during 2010. It excludes all permanently out of camp. Rations are provided only to those personally attending distributions and actual feeding figures are typically 4% lower than the caseload.
2. UNHCR figure includes registered, pending PAB and some students but excludes new arrivals.
3. Includes Kayan

Fig. 3.1 Population figures of temporary shelters along the Thai–Myanmar Border as per July 2010. *Source* TBBC, at: http://www.tbbc.org/temporaryshelters/2010-07-jul-map-tbbc-unhcr.pdf

3.1.3 Case Studies

At present, there are about 140,000 Myanmar refugees living in nine border camps in Thailand. Many of them have been there for nearly 20 years. These refugees are under the protection of UNHCR and depend on subsistence-level humanitarian assistance provided by various NGOs under the agreement of the RTG. This humanitarian assistance is provided to the refugees under various restrictive conditions. The overcrowded housing conditions, which result from camp consolidation and increasing population numbers, have led to the deterioration of the camps' environment. Waste problems, pollution, disease and inadequate access to clean water have been on the rise. Long-term confinement in this kind of environment, the lack of space for recreational and educational purposes, restrictions on mobility and limited access to employment and higher education have had a significant negative impact on refugees' potential for development. This often also results in a series of environmental problems for the nearby hosting communities. Such problems include contaminated water supply, reduced access to forest products and soil and river bank erosion. There is a strong need to understand the impact of displaced people's temporary shelter on the surrounding environment in more detail. To generate such understanding, the environmental impacts were studied in three temporary shelters: Tham Hin Temporary Shelter in Ratchaburi Province; Baan Mai Nai Soi Temporary Shelter in Mae Hong Son Province and Mae La Temporary Shelter in Tak Province.

3.2 The Environmental Situation in the Displaced Persons' Temporary Settlements

3.2.1 Tham Hin, Ratchaburi Province

3.2.1.1 Location and Access

Baan Tham Hin Temporary Shelter is located in a valley named Hub Kraton (Suan Phueng Local Administration Organisation 2010). It is located in Moo 5, Baan Tham Him, Tambon Suan Phueng, Amphoe Suan Phueng, approximately 10 km from the Thai–Myanmar borders near Amya Pass, about 20 km away from Amphoe Suan Phueng and circa 60 km from Suan Phueng LAO Division in the province of Ratchaburi. Tham Hin Temporary Shelter covers an area of approximately 40 rai or 6.4 hect. Access to the shelter is by a 4 m wide asphalt road located south of the shelter. From the shelter it is about 3 km to Baan Tham Hin Health Station via route 4019 from where there are two alternative routes to nearby communities. In addition, there is an unpaved road leading from the shelter to the Thai–Myanmar border at Baan Tako Pid Thong (Figs. 3.2 and 3.3).

3.2.1.2 Population

The majority of the displaced persons in Baan Tham Him Temporary Shelter are from Myanmar and a minority of them were born in Thailand. Some 96.5 % of them originate from Tavoy, which is located on the border near Kanchanaburi and Ratchaburi Provinces. The rest is from Ayeyarwady, Bago, Rangoon, Mon and Rakhine. Approximately 95 % of the shelter populations are Karen, 1 % are Myanmar and 4 % have other nationalities (TBBC) the population of the Baan Tham Hin shelter. Over the past few years. 201 in 5,111 to 2007 in 7,959 has steadily decreased from 0 (Table 3.1).

Fig. 3.2 Location of Baan Tham Hin Temporary Shelter. *Source* The authors

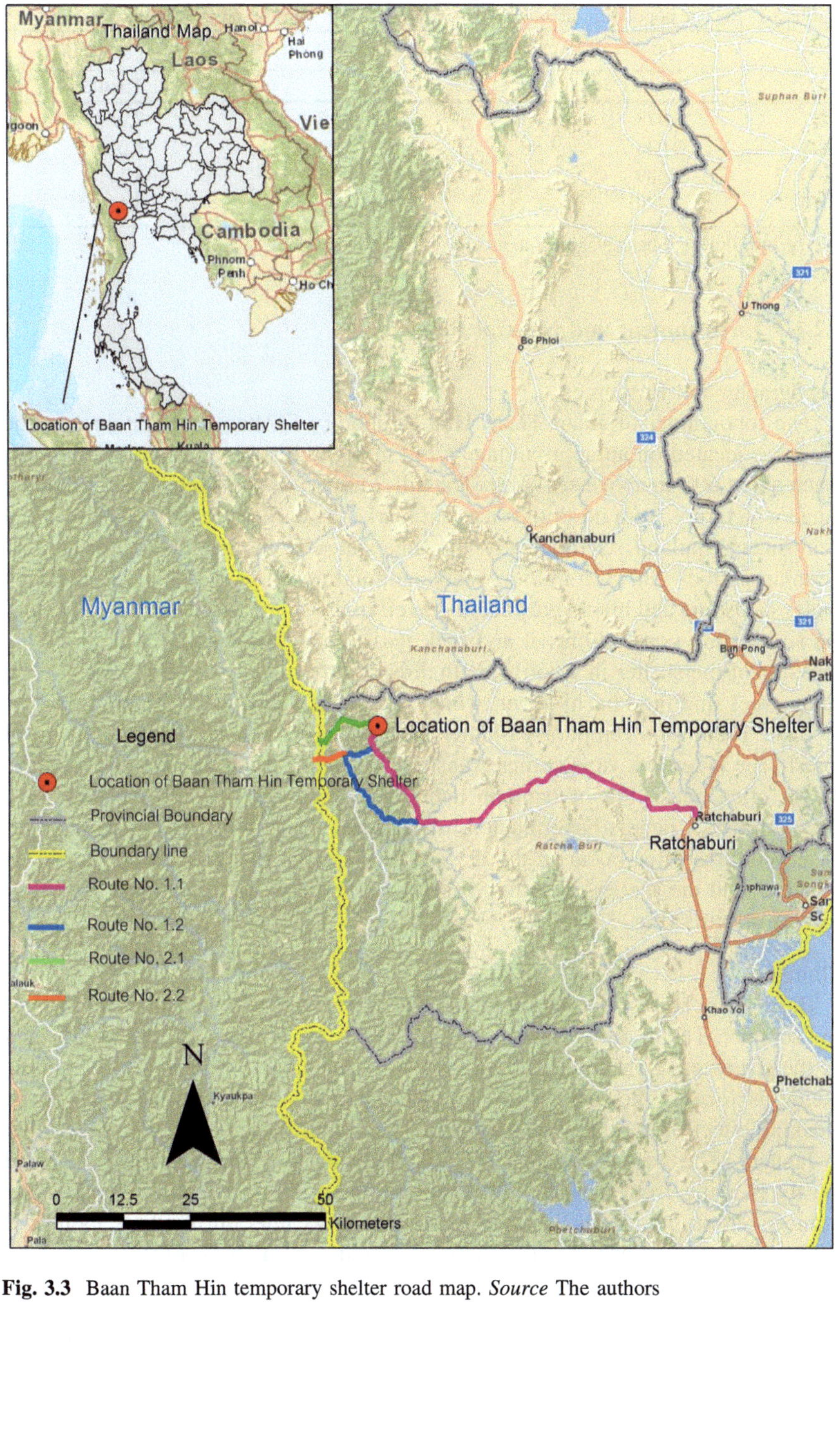

Fig. 3.3 Baan Tham Hin temporary shelter road map. *Source* The authors

Table 3.1 Recent population developments in Baan Tham Hin temporary shelter

Year	Number of population in Tham Hin temporary shelter		
	Male	Female	Total
2007	3,978	3,981	7,959
2008	3,044	2,969	6,013
2009	2,589	2,522	5,111
2010	2,589	2,522	5,111

Source http://www.tbbc.org/camps/populations.htm

3.2.1.3 Environment and Natural Resources

Topography and Resources

The topography of Baan Tham Hin Temporary Shelter is mountainous. The shelter is located on an approximately 240 m high hillside. Surrounding summits reach about 600-m above sea level. The hills are part of the Tanintharyi Mountain range which runs from north to south and marks the border between Myanmar and Peninsular Thailand. Geologically the area dates from the Carboniferous and Permian periods 280–320 million years ago, and is comprised of black and grey shale, sandstone and black–grey shale gravel. In the shelter itself the first 25 cm of the soil mainly consists of soil and rock mass. Huay Klum creek runs along the east side of the shelter in a north–south direction, formed by the small Huay Nam Khun creek and the Phachi River, which meet at Amphoe Suan Phueng.

Baan Tham Hin Temporary Shelter is surrounded with deciduous and mixed forest. The latter is a vegetational transition between sparse forest and deciduous forest, often consisting of bamboo and rubberwood among other species. In a narrow hillside, people have planted rubber trees, eucalyptus trees, corn and tapioca. Wildfires often occur in the dry season. Various species of wildlife can be found around the shelter, including barking dears, dears, small animals and many species of birds (Fig. 3.4).

Climate

Baan Tham Hin Temporary Shelter experiences three seasons: monsoon, winter and summer. The monsoon season lasts from May to October. The area is affected by the southwest monsoon that blows from the Andaman Sea. The area where the shelter is located, however, does not receive a lot of rainfall because of the blocking effect of Tanintharyi Mountain. The winter season lasts from December to January. The weather can get quite cold during these months, with the wind mostly blowing from a north easterly direction. Rainfall is sparse. Finally, the summer season lasts from February to April. The weather during these months is hot and dry, with temperatures sometimes reaching as high as 40 °C.

Natural Disasters

Baan Tham Hin Temporary Shelter faces risks from earthquakes, floods, and forest and brushfires. The highest earthquake recorded in Kanchanaburi measured

Fig. 3.4 Topography of Baan Tham Hin Temporary Shelter. *Source* Photo by study team

5.9 on the Richter scale. Earthquakes are considered dangerous in the area in particular because of their capacity to trigger landslides in the hills and mountains. Flood risks in the Huay Klum river basin area, where the shelter is located, are increasing because of deforestation. Forest and brushfires occur in the summer season and are capable of causing great damage. They are caused by humans and sometimes by nature (Figs. 3.5, 3.6).

Flora and Fauna

The most important types of vegetation that are found in the mixed forest area are *Shorea obtusa* Wall. ex Blume, *Shorea siamensis* Miq and *Pterocarpus macrocarpus*. Along the hillside, *Bambusa arundinacea* Willd and *Bambusa*

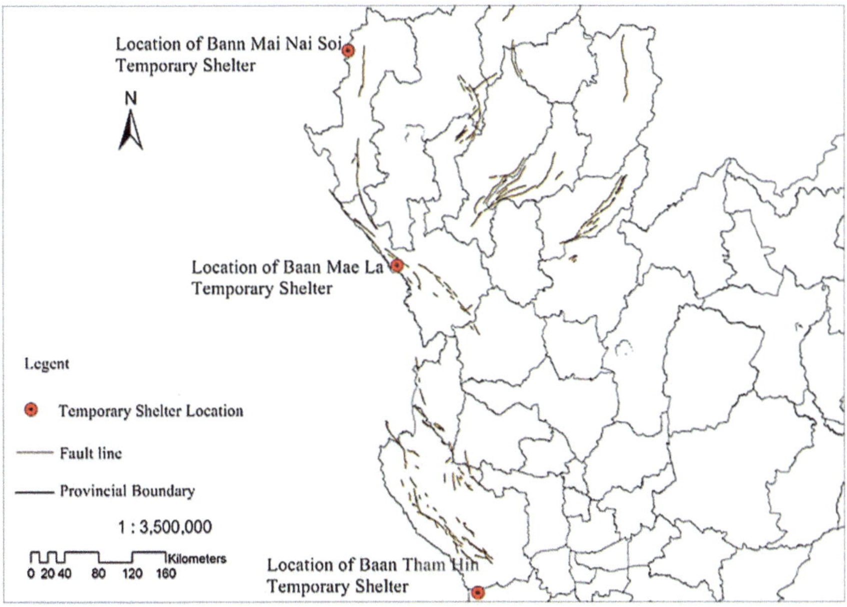

Fig. 3.5 Fault lines in the earth surface around Baan Tham Hin temporary shelter. *Source* The authors

Fig. 3.6 Topography of Baan Tham Hin temporary shelter. *Source* The authors

nutans alternate with degraded forest and agriculture area. Various species of wildlife can be found around the evergreen forest on Thailand–Myanmar border are elephant, barking deer, common serow, wild boar, mouse deer, langur, gibbon, gallus and birds (Suan Phueng Local Administration Organisation 2010).

Settlement and Local Communities

As noted, most of the area consists of mountainous terrain and narrow strips of lowlands along the creeks between the mountains. These lowlands have fertile soils and have traditionally attracted more settlements than the highlands. They are a mix of plantations, sparse forests and settlements, most of which are located near the main routes of transportation. Most settlements started as a collection of small houses. These would typically develop into a small village, and later on into larger communities. Around such communities developed agricultural areas. Today still, the majority of the people living in the area are farmers. Crop products include pomelo, longan, jackfruit, mango, sweet tamarind, jujube, bananas and lettuce. Farm products are tapioca, sugar cane, eucalyptus and neem. Suan Phueng Local Administrative Organisation is divided into eight divisions. The first people who settled in the area were Karen who used to work in the mine. Currently, the population amounts to 10,235 people, slightly more males, in 4,241 households (Fig. 3.7).

Baan Tham Hin Temporary Shelter was found in 1997 to host displaced persons fleeing from war in Myanmar. It is located on Moo 5, Baan Tham Hin, Tambon Suan Phueng, Amphoe Suan Phueng, approximately 10 km from the Thai–Myanmar borders. The shelter covers an area of approximately 40 rai. The topography of Baan Tham Hin Temporary Shelter is mountainous that alternate with narrow hillsides, which run from north to south. The hills are part of the Tanintharyi mountain range that marks the border between Thailand and Myanmar borders. Huay Klum creek runs alongside the shelter (Table 3.2).

Baan Tham Hin Temporary Shelter is surrounded with sparse forest that alternate with degraded forest and agriculture area. There are only a few species of wildlife that found around Thailand–Myanmar borders due to wildlife hunting along the shelter area. Access to the shelter is by Highway 3208 that connects to Highway 4, the Phetkasem Road, to access Amphur Muang, Ratchaburi Province. It is also connected to Highway 3087, the Ratchaburi–Papok Road, to get to Amphoe Suan Phueng before turning into Route 4019, which is an asphalt road that passes through police checkpoint 7 at Baan Takobon and leads to Baan Tham Hin Temporary Shelter.

Most of the area consists of mountainous terrain and narrow strips of lowlands along the creeks between the mountains. Due to the limitation of the physical space, these lowlands attracted more group settlement than the highlands. There are a mix of plantation and settlement. Around such communities developed agriculture areas. Today still, the majority of the people living in the area are farmers. Crop products include pomelo, longan, jackfruit, mango, sweet tamarind, jujube, bananas and lettuce. Farm products are tapioca, sugar cane, eucalyptus and neem.

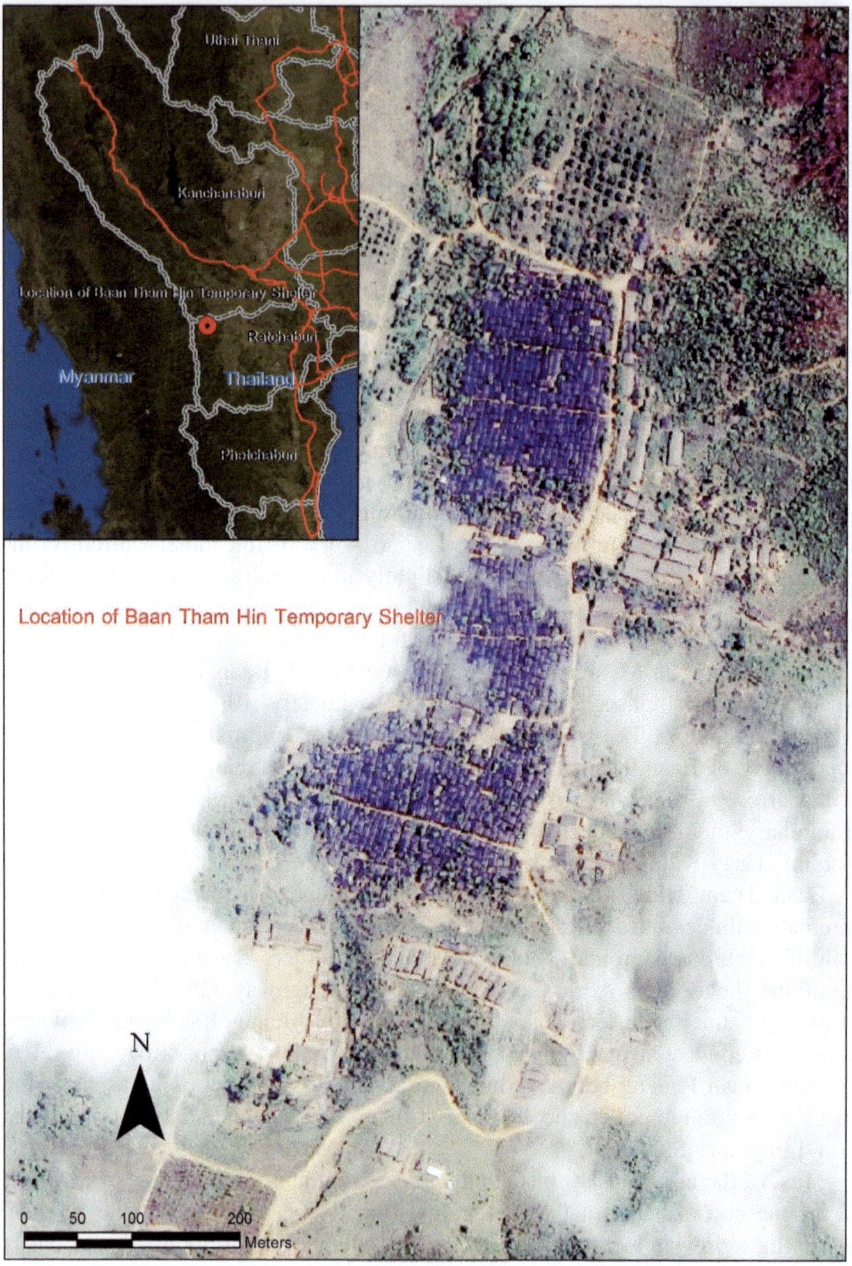

Fig. 3.7 Baan Tham Hin Temporary Shelter settlement. *Source* The authors

Table 3.2 Villages and their population in Suan Phueng Local Administration Organisation

Village no.	Name of the village	Male	Female	Total	No. of households
1	Baan Boa	187	137	324	156
2	Baan Thung Feak	577	502	1,079	384
3	Baan Papok	1,553	1,424	2,977	1,410
4	Baan Na Khun Seang	173	162	335	130
5	Baan Tham Hin	453	417	870	358
6	Baan Huay Klum	327	280	607	223
7	Baan Huay Pak	942	912	1,854	865
8	Baan Tako Lang	1,133	1,056	2,189	715
	Total	5,345	4,890	10,235	4,241

Source Suan Phueng Local Administration Organisation, 3 Year Development Plan 2011–2013 Suan Phueng Local Administration Organisation: Amphoe Suan Phueng, Ratchaburi Province 2010

Baan Tham Hin Temporary Shelter is located in Suan Phueng Local Administration Organisation, which divided into eight divisions. The area is home to 10,235 people; 5,345 male, 4,890 female and 4,241 households. The majority of the displaced persons in the Baan Tham Hin Temporary Shelter are from Myanmar. Some 96.5 % of them originate from Tavoy. Approximately, 95 % of the shelter populations are Karen, 1 % are Myanmar and 4 % have other nationalities.

3.2.2 *Baan Mai Nai Soi, Mae Hong Son Province*

3.2.2.1 Location and Access

Baan Mai Nai Soi Temporary Shelter is located in Pa Mae Pai National Park. The shelter covers an area of 1,600 rai (256 hect.) in Nai Soi Village at Moo 4, Tambon Pangmoo, Amphur, Mae Hong Son Province. The topography of the shelter consists of lowland areas in a forest protection zone of Nai Soi National Park on the right bank of Pai River. The shelter is located 2 km from the Thai–Myanmar border. There are two paths between Thailand and Myanmar: Tana Kwai path and Doi Seang path. The second path is divided into two routes: Baan Pang Kwai and Baan Pang Tractor. They are approximately 40 km from Mae Hong Son and take about a 1.15 h drive. Baan Mai Nai Soi is furthermore connected with Huay Nam Soi to the north, Lam Huay Phong to the south and Baan Nai Soi Thai to the east (Fig. 3.8).

3.2.2.2 Population

The population of displaced persons in the Baan Mae La Temporary Shelter mainly consists of Red Karen. They make up 94 % of the total population,

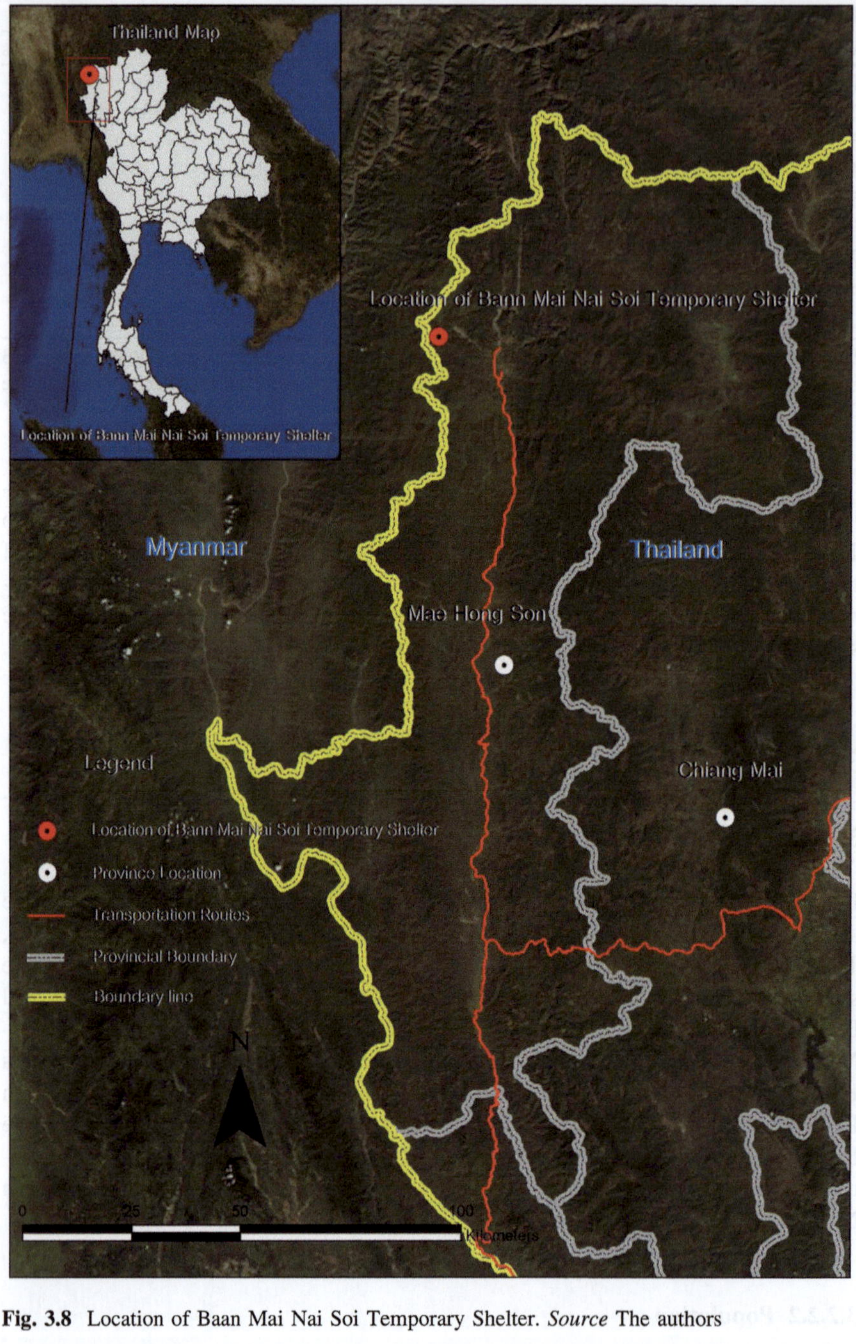

Fig. 3.8 Location of Baan Mai Nai Soi Temporary Shelter. *Source* The authors

followed by 3 % of Karen and 3 % of other nationalities. In recent years, the shelter population has decreased from almost 20,000 in 2007 to 13,319 in 2010 (Table 3.3).

3.2.2.3 Environment and Natural Resources

Topography

Mae Hong Son is dominated by high mountains and home to rich natural forests. Most of these forests, some 88 %, are part of National Park that covers approximately 6,976,650 rai. The area's mountain ranges run from north to south and parallel to each other. One of the more well-known mountains is the Dan Lao mountain range, located in the north of Mae Hong Son, which forms a division between Thailand and Myanmar. Another well-known mountain is the Tanon Thongchai mountain range which divides into two ranges, namely the West Tanon Thongchai mountain range, the borderline between Thailand and Myanmar and the East Tanon Thongchai mountain range, the borderline between Mae Hong Son and Chaing Mai Province. The highest point in the Tanon Thongchai mountain range is the summit of Mae Ya, located in East Tanon Thongchai mountain range at 2005 m above sea level (Mae Hong Son Province Study Report). The geological resources are composed of gravel, sandstone, shale, slate, chert rock and limestone, and date back to the Carboniferous period 290–335 million years ago. The area's soil consists of a 100–150 cm deep slope complex consisting of soil and gravel. The soil has a very high drainage capacity.

Baan Mae La Temporary Shelter is cut in two by Huay Pong creek. The shelter is located in the Pai River Wildlife Protection area. The area contains rich vegetation for wildlife due to its undulation terrain. The area comprises two types of forests. The first type is tropical rainforest with brandisiana, lithocarpus bennetti, cinnamon, betula alnoides buch and pine trees in some areas. As for the ground cover plants, there are many species of ferns, orchids and mos. This type of forest usually grows in the watershed area. Another type of forest found in Baan Mai Soi Temporary Shelter area is mixed forest alternating with sparse forest. There are many more species of bamboos located in various locations of the region, especially in the lowland and hillside areas. These species of trees will shed their leaves during the dry season of the year.

Table 3.3 Recent population development in Baan Mai Nai Soi temporary shelter

Year	Number of population in Baan Mai Nai Soi Temporary Shelter		
	Male	Female	Total
2007	10,218	9,455	19,673
2008	9,731	9,190	18,921
2009	9,536	10,046	19,582
2010	6,777	6,542	13,319

Source http://www.tbbc.org/camps/populations.htm

Since Mae Pai River Wildlife Protection area contains many water resources and food supplies, wildlife is abundant, especially in the deep forest. Due to improvements in transportation in the area, people and hill tribes move in and out of the area with increasing ease. Some of them hunt the wild animals for goods and products, causing wild animals to migrate into Myanmar, and resulting in decreasing numbers of wildlife. Some important types of wildlife are barking deer, deer, boar, chamois, goral, gibbon, palm civet, porcupine, pheasant, tiger and bear (Fig. 3.9).

Climate

Mae Hong Son has a hot and humid climate. It experiences very high temperatures in the summer months of February to May, over 40 °C, very low temperatures in the winter from November to February and heavy rainfall in the monsoon season from May to October. Moreover, Mae Hong Son is frequently covered in fog because of its high location in mountainous terrain.

Forestry

Baan Mai Nai Soi Temporary Shelter is located in the lower right part of a National Park and home to rich natural forests, which include evergreen and mixed forests. The types of vegetation that are found in the area are ferns and caladiums. Evergreen forest is found in the highland area, 600–800 m above sea level. Vegetation includes red rubberwood, jambolan plum, fig and queen's flowers. Mixed forest has an economic significant value, especially if it contains teak wood trees. This type of forest will spread in the wide area in a highland. The important types of vegetations that are found in the area are teak wood trees, Burmese rosewood, Iron wood and Dipterocarpus. Various types of bamboos that are found in the area are Dendrocalamus stricutus and Bambusa nutan.

Since Mae Pai River Wildlife Protection area contains many water resources and food supplied, wildlife is abundant, especially in the deep forest. Due to improvement in transportation in the area, people and hill tribes move in and out of the area with increasing ease. Some of them hunt the wild animals for goods and products, causing wild animals to migrate into Myanmar, and resulting in decreasing numbers of wildlife. There are only a few small species of wild

Fig. 3.9 Topography of Baan Mai Nai Soi temporary shelter. *Source* Photo by study team

animals, Gallus gallus and Pysnonotus jocosus, found in the area while the large species of wild animals has been disappeared. The wildlife in the area has become extinct (Community leaders, interviewed on 1 August 2010).

The current issue that occurs in the area is deforestation. Teak and bamboo trees were cut down for timber products and food supplies. Disforestation has spread wilder and the trees do not grow fast enough for people needs which then causes ecosystem imbalanced and conflicted over natural resources between local people who live in the area and displaced persons (Fig. 3.10).

3.2.2.4 Settlement and Local Communities

Mae Hong Son Province is situated in a highland area. The slopes run from west to east and contain rich forests and watersheds. The lowland areas are located along the rivers and are suitable for human settlement. The settlements are located along the main rivers, which include the Pai River, the Sa Nga River and the Soi River. The lowland areas also used for agriculture. Farm crops include rice, soy bean, groundnut, garlic and sesame. In the highland areas, there are rice fields on the hillside and the slopes (Tambon Pang Moo Local Administration Organisation 2011). Baan Mai Nai Soi Temporary Shelter is located in Tambon Pang Moo LAO Division. This division is divided into 13 villages comprising of male and female populations (Table 3.4).

Baan Mai Nai Soi is located in the lower right of Pa Mae Pai National Park, Nai Soi Village, Moo 4, Tambon Pang Moo, Amphur Maung, Mae Hong Son Province. The topography of the shelter consists of lowland areas in a forest protection zone of Nai Soi National part on the right bank of Pai River, 2 km from Thailand–Myanmar borders. Another type of topography that is found in the area is complex highland. Baan Mai Nai Soi is furthermore connected with Huay Phong creek to the north and located approximately 800 m from the main stream in the mountain. The creek runs in the north to south direction and meets with another creek at the south part of the shelter approximately 1.5 km.

Baan Mai Nai Soi is situated in a hot and humid climate. It experiences very high temperatures in the summer, very low temperatures in the winter and heavy rainfall in the monsoon season. It is frequently covered in fog because of its high location in mountainous terrain.

Baan Mai Nai Soi Temporary Shelter's surrounding area comprises two types of rich forests, which include evergreen and mixed forests. The types of vegetation found in the watershed area are ferns and caladiums. Dipterocarpus is found in the area, the leaves from which are used to make rooves which last 4–5 years. Currently, there are a large number of wildlife hunting which causes the decreasing number of wild animals. There are only a few small species of wild animals found in the area while the large species of wild animals has been disappeared. The wildlife in the area has become extinct.

Access to the shelter is by driving along the Asian Highway Network to Nakornsawan, Kampengphet and Lampang Provinces. Then, drive on the Highway

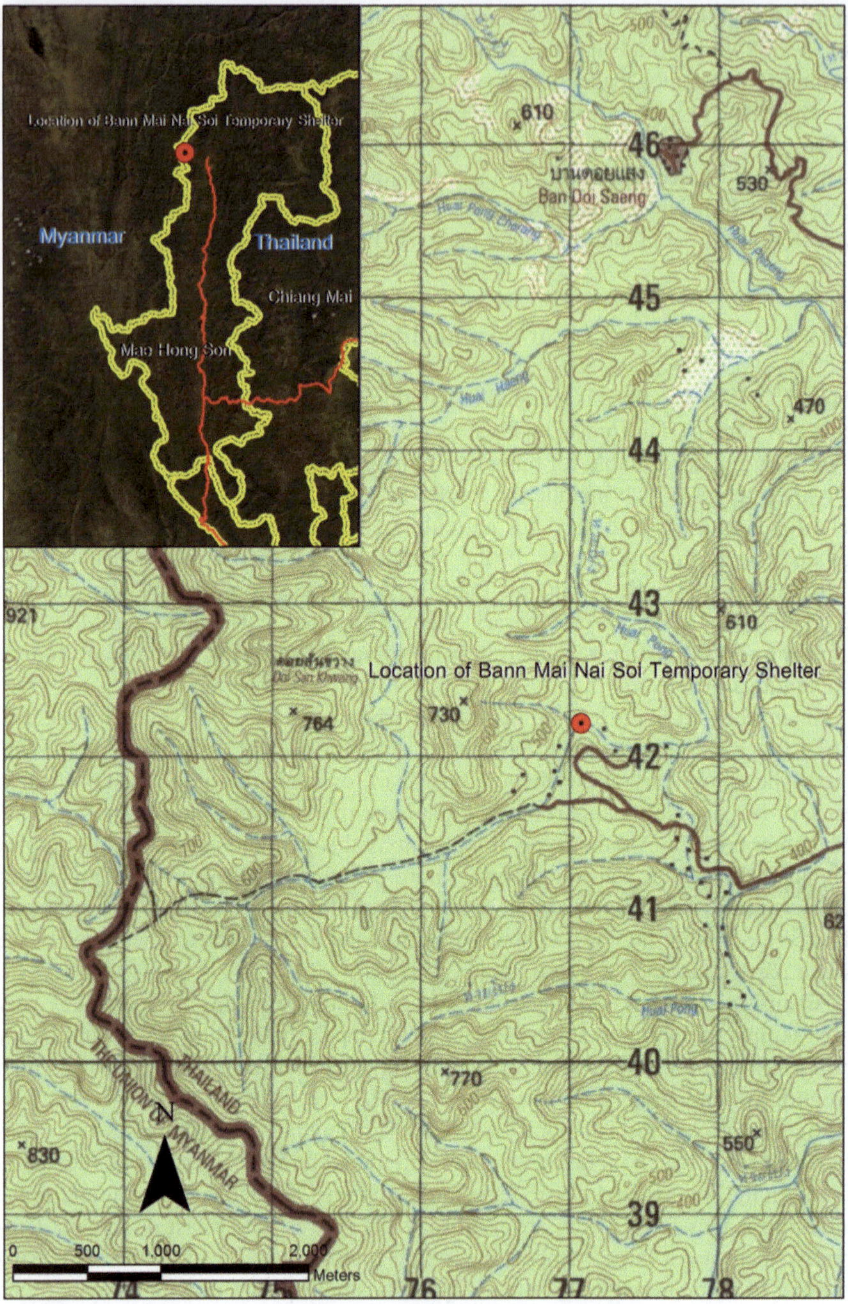

Fig. 3.10 Topography of Baan Mai NaiSoi temporary shelter. *Source* The authors

Table 3.4 Villages and their population in Mae La Local Administration Organisation

Village no.	Village name	Male	Female	Total	No. of households
1	Baan Pang Moo	1,247	1,099	2,346	1,037
2	Baan Kung Mai Sak	608	543	1,151	427
3	Baan Tung Kong Mou	545	470	1,015	477
4	Baan Nai Soi	829	865	1,694	568
5	Baan Baan Mai	548	562	1,110	619
6	Baan Sob Pong	459	469	938	316
7	Baan Sob Soey	424	394	818	280
8	Baan Mai Ngae	819	801	1,620	846
9	Baan Mai Sa Pae	350	305	655	171
10	BaanPa Kho Low	170	169	339	109
11	Baan Khun Klang	534	581	1,115	609
12	Baan Chan Muang	484	491	975	711
13	Baan Doi Seang	191	151	342	85
	Total	7,367	7,032	14,399	6,251

Source Pang Moo Local Administrative Organisation, 3-Year Development Plan 2011–2014, Pang Moo Local Administration Organisation: Amphur Mae Hong Son, Mae Hong Son Province 2010

1 to Chiang Mai Province. From Chiang Mai, use the Chiang Mai–Chiang Dao route to get to Amphur Mae Tang–Amphur Pai on Highway 107. After that turn left on Highway 1095, known locally as Mae Malai–Pai route to Mae Tang. Drive along Highway 1095 to Amphur Pai and Amphur Bang MaPa, Mae Hong Son Province. Then, go straight to Baan Pang Moo and cross Mae Nam Pai Bridge at milepost no. 199. Turn left on Accelerated Rural Development (ARD) Road and follow the road approximately 1 km to a tri-section road. Turn left into Baan Nai Soi ARD Road. Follow the road approximately 17 km to Wat Baan Nai Sot. There is an intersection located 500 m away.

3.2.3 Mae La Temporary Shelter, Tak Province

3.2.3.1 Location and Access

Baan Mae La Temporary Shelter is located in Tak Province, in Moo 9, Tombon Mae La, Amphur Tha Song Yang. It lies 10 km from the Thai–Myanmar border and 60 km from Amphur Mae Sot. The nearest village is Baan Mae La Moo 9 which is located 1 km from the shelter. Baan Mae La Temporary Shelter is located on Route 105, which connects Amphur Mae Sot with Amphur Mae Sarieng in Mae Hong Son Province. The mountain range west of the shelter forms the division between Myanmar and Thailand. The shelter covers 184 hect., about 1,150 rai.

Mae La is connected with the Paru creek and the Doi Paru mountain ridge to the north, to Route 105 to the east, the road from Amphur Mae Sot to Amphur Mae

Sarieng, to Amphur Mae Ramad and Amphur Tha Song Yang to the south via private plantations, and to Doi Lawa and Doi Parue to the west. The latter forms a 3.7 km natural barrier.

The shelter can be reached by car, motorcycle and on foot, although this does not mean access is easy. Local pathways have been created around the shelter to enable mobility between the shelter and surrounding villages. Since the shelter is located in a National Park, in a protected forest area, it is difficult for the shelter population to transport their products to any markets (Fig. 3.11).

3.2.3.2 Population

Currently, there are 31,439 registered displaced persons in the shelter, with another 20,000 displaced persons from Myanmar waiting to be registered. About 97 % of the shelter population is Karen, 2 % is Myanmar and 1 % other nationalities (Table 3.5).

3.2.3.3 Environment and Natural Resource

Topography

Baan Mae La Temporary Shelter is located in Tha Song Yang National Park. The landscape is dominated by fairly high mountains that alternate with narrow valleys. The mountains are part of the Thanon Thongchai mountain range. The shelter is located at about 200 m above sea level while mountain peaks in the area reach 700–800 m high. Geologically, the area dates back 140–200 million years. Its geological resources are composed of sandstone, sandstone powder and limestone. The soil on which the shelter itself is built has good drainage capacity.

Baan Mae La Temporary Shelter is situated on the banks of the Huay Si Mo Kue creek, at the point where it is joined by the Huay Paru creek and the Huay Pa Toey creek.

The shelter finds itself in a protected forest area comprising dry evergreen forest. The most important types of vegetation are red rubberwood and makharmong. The lower parts of the National Park contain sparse forest. There are rice fields in the lowlands and plantations or natural forest in the uplands (Fig. 3.12).

Climate

Baan Mae La Temporary Shelter experiences three seasons. Summer season lasts from March to April. Temperatures typically range from 28 to 33 °C and rainfall is sparse. Monsoon season lasts from May to October. August sees the heaviest rainfall and temperatures range from 19 to 29 °C. Winter season lasts from November to February. Temperatures range from 15 to 25 °C and rainfall is again sparse (Mae La Local Administration Organisation 2009).

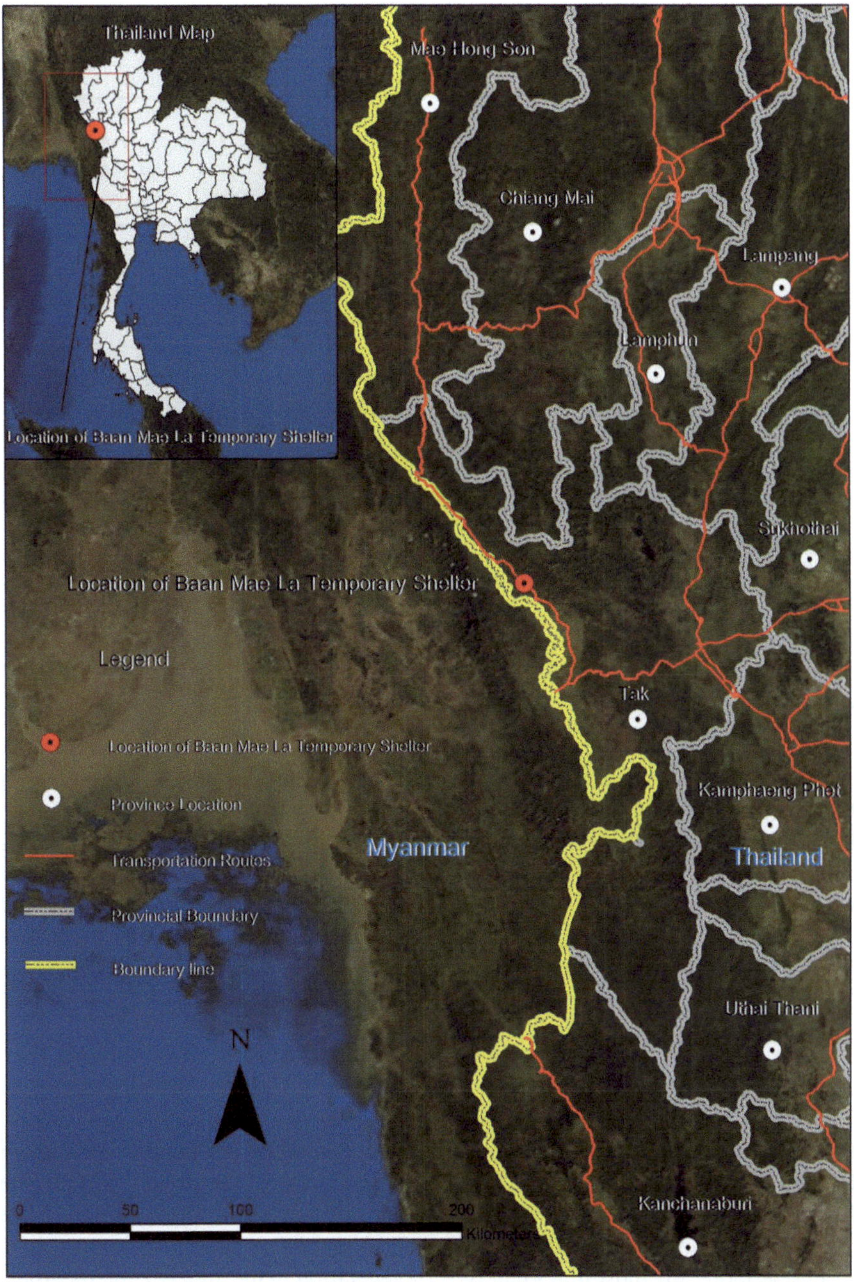

Fig. 3.11 Location of Mae La temporary shelter. *Source* The authors

Table 3.5 Recent population developments in Baan Mae La Temporary Shelter

Year	Number of population in Baan Mae La Temporary shelter		
	Male	Female	Total
2007	25,236	24,124	49,363
2008	19,638	19,297	38,935
2009	16,804	16,764	33,568
2010	15,504	15,602	31,100

Source http://www.tbbc.org/camps/populations.htm

Fig. 3.12 Topography of Baan Mae La Temporary Shelter. *Source* Photo taken by study team

Natural Disasters

Baan Mae La Temporary Shelter faces risks from three types of disasters: earthquakes, floods and forest and brushfires. The shelter finds itself near a faulting line and thus may be prone to earthquakes. Flooding risks in the area are increasing because of ongoing deforestation and land clearing for land development, agriculture and the extraction of timber products. Heavy rainfall in the monsoon season occasionally causes flooding. In contrast, summer season sees frequent and damaging forest and brush fires caused by humans and sometimes by nature (Fig. 3.13).

Forestry

Baan Mae La Temporary Shelter is located in Tha Song Yang National Park comprising of dry evergreen forest. This type of forest is usually found in 300–600 m above sea level along the hillside. The types of vegetation that is found in the area are Hopea Ferrea Lanness, Lagerstroemia floribunda, Anisoptera Costata Korth, Dipterocarpus Alatus Roxb.ex G. Don. The lower part of the National Park contains sparse forest. The types of vegetation that is found in the area are Bamboos, Rattans and Ferns.

Furthermore, the most important type of vegetation in the area is Dipterocarpus. This type of vegetation is found in the mixed forest area 100–600 m above sea level. Dipterocarpus' leaf is similar to teak leaf, but a little bit thicker. This specie of tree will shed it leaves in winter season of the year. The leaves are used for roofing, which will last 4–5 years.

Fig. 3.13 Topography of Baan Mae La temporary shelter. *Source* The authors

There are a few species of wildlife that are used to be found in the area, which include barking deer, deer, wild boar, common serow, pangolin and Bengal monitor (Mae La Local Administration Organisation 2010).

The current situation of natural resources around Baan Mae La Temporary Shelter has been critical. The forest and wildlife are continually destroyed and hunted, especially along Baan Mae Ook Hue Village. The large trees were cut down to make timber products and coal (Mae La Local Administration Organisation 2010). In addition, a large number of bamboo trees were cut down by displaced persons, which cause the food supplied shortage for the local people. This is because the bamboo trees do not grow back fast enough for the local people needs. The current conflict between the local people and displaced persons focuses on Dipterocarpus' leaves collecting. Both the local people and displaced persons use the leaves to fix their house and for sale, which then cause the supplies shortage (Mae La Local Administration Organisation 2009).

Settlement and Local Communities

Most of the settlements in the area are located in the lowlands, along hillside or near natural water resources. Due to the limited availability of agricultural land, the lowlands mostly see seasonal rice fields that alternate with vegetation and fruit orchards. The highlands are home to plantations of soy bean and corn. There are only a few chicken, pig, buffalo, duck, goat and elephant farms in the area.

The study area is situated in Tambon Mae La LAO Division, which is divided into 12 villages. The majority of the population is Thai with Karen nationality. The area is home to 7,566 people, recorded in September 2009, 2,734and households. The major religion is Buddhism, comprising 95 % of the total population (Table 3.6, Fig. 3.14).

Baan Mae La Temporary Shelter was founded in 1984. The majority of the population is Karen who fled from home during the war in southwest Myanmar to Thailand during 1984–1996. The shelter is located in Moo 9 Tambon Mae La, Amphur Tha Song Yang, Tak Province, 10 km from Thailand–Myanmar border, circa 80 km from Tak Province. The landscape is dominated by fairly high mountains that alternate with narrow valleys. The mountains are part of Thanon Thongchai mountain range. Amphur Tha Song Yang is located in the area, reaching more than 300 m high. Because the area is part of Thanon Thongchai mountain range and affected by southwest monsoon winds that blow from the Andaman Sea, the weather in the area consists of tropical monsoon climate and a heavy rainfall almost all year long, with high risk of flooding in the monsoon season.

Baan Mae La Temporary Shelter is situated in dry evergreen forest. This type of forest is usually found in 300–600 m above sea level along the hillside. The most important type of vegetation in the area is Dipterocarpus, with its leaves used for roofing. Currently, there is no wildlife around the shelter due to wildlife hunting for human food supplies.

Baan Mae La Temporary Shelter is hard to access and difficult for people to transport their products to the markets because it is located in a fairly high mountain far from the main transportation. The shelter is located on Route 105, which is a two-way road that connects Amphur Mae Sot with Amphur Mae

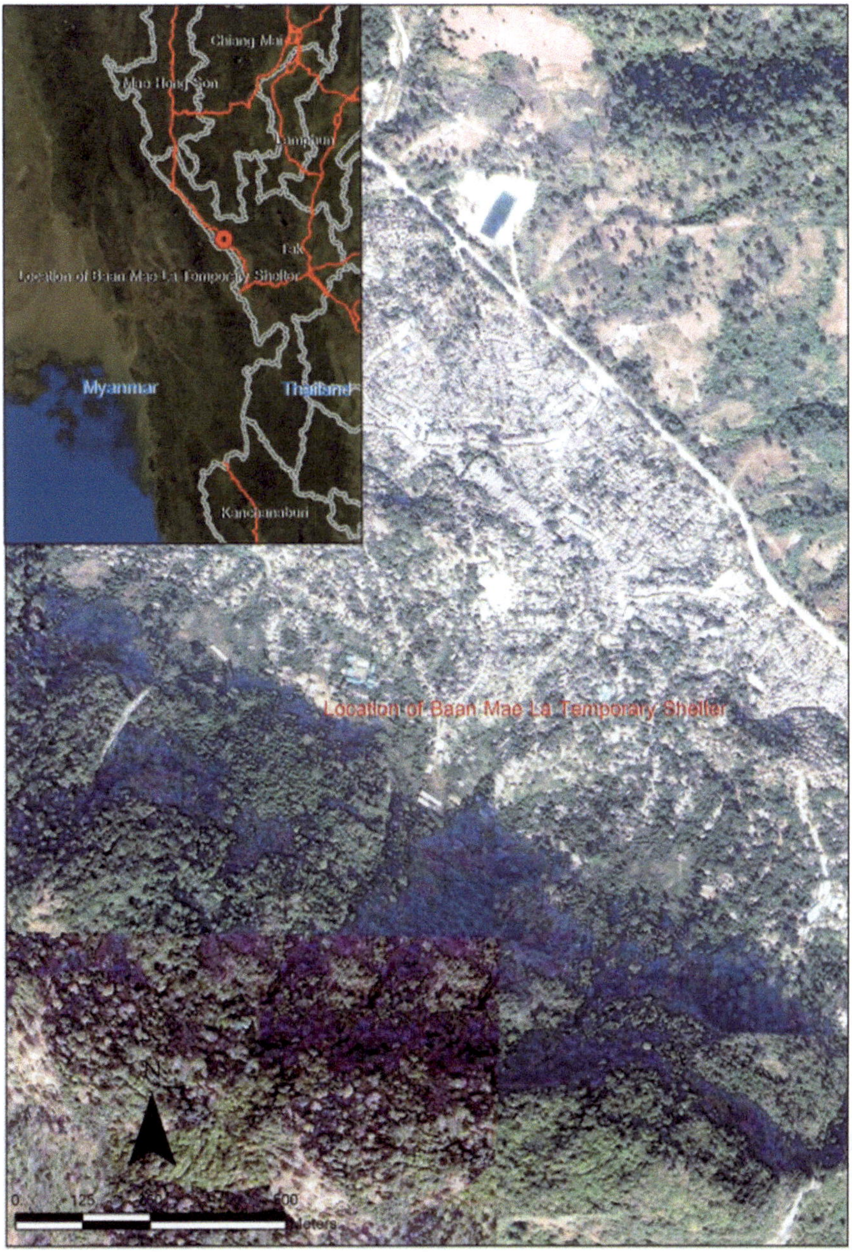

Fig. 3.14 Baan Mae La temporary shelter settlement. *Source* The authors

Table 3.6 Villages and their population in Mae La Local Administration Organisation

Village no.	Village name	Male	Female	Total	No. of households
1	Baan Mae La Thai	295	288	583	210
2	Baan Mae La Yang	662	692	1,354	469
3	Baan Mae Ook Parue	257	270	527	210
4	Baan Huay Nokkok	248	245	493	231
5	Baan Kamapado	591	558	1,149	462
6	Baan Kamapado	368	348	716	247
7	Baan Khun Huay Nokkok	294	279	573	199
8	BaanTee Jue Lo Kee	194	187	381	123
9	Baan Mae Ook Hue	167	176	343	151
10	Baan Panokkee	270	302	572	235
11	Baan Mae La Pokee	148	130	278	58
12	Baan Mae La Kee	319	278	597	139
	Total	3,813	3,753	7,566	2,734

Source Mae La Local Administration Organisation, 3-year Development Plan 2011–2014, Mae La Local Administration Organisation: Amphur Tha Song Yang, Tak Province 2011

Sarieng. Most of the settlements in the area are located in the lowlands, along hillside. The lowlands mostly see seasonal rice fields that alternate with vegetation and fruit orchards. There are only a few chicken, pig, buffalo, duck, goat and elephant farms in the area.

The study area is situated in Tambon Mae la LAO Division, which is divided into 12 villages. The majority of the population is Thai with Karen nationality. The area is home to 7,566 people, 3,813 male and 3,753 female and 2,734 households. The major religion is Buddhism, 95 % of the total population. Currently, there are 31,439 registered displaced persons in the shelters. Another 20,000 displaced persons from Myanmar are waiting to be registered in the shelter. About 97 % of the shelter population is Karen, 2 % is Myanmar and 1 % has other nationality.

Baan Tham Hin, Baan Mai Nai Soi and Baan Mae La Temporary Shelters are all located near the Thailand–Myanmar border, the key factor in provision of sanctuary from war in Myanmar. The shelters are situated along Thanon Thongchai and Tenasserim Ranges. These two ranges formed the division between Thailand and Myanmar borders.

The study shows that the Temporary Shelters are located in the mountainous terrains. The topographies of the areas are complex highland, which experiences high temperatures in the summer season, very low temperatures in the winter season and heavy rainfall in the monsoon season. Flooding risks in the areas are caused by heavy rainfall and watershed settlements. The areas are covered with rich natural forests and contain many water resources to the nearby communities. There are a few creeks run along the shelters. Displaced persons can rely on forest and water supplies for living. These factors are significant for displaced persons to choose the location of the shelter.

The majority of the displaced persons are from Tavoy, Ayeyarwady, Bago, Rangon, Karen and Rakhine in Myanmar which are located near to the Thailand borders. Most of the populations in the shelters are Karen, Red Karen and the minorities are other nationalities, such as Myanmar. The numbers of male and female populations are almost equal. The religions that are found in the shelters are Buddhism, Christian and worshipping spirit. There are a few people in Baan Mae La Temporary Shelter who are Muslim.

Although the shelters are located in the mountainous terrain and covered with forests, they are easy to access. This is because there are routes that were built for the NGOs to transport products and goods to the shelters.

There are various types of natural resources in the shelter areas, which include many species of Thai vegetation including Hopea Odorata, Burma Padauk, Teak wood and Dipterocarpus. The areas have important ecosystems and biodiversity. The study shows that the forests around the shelters have been destroyed in a widespread area and are likely to expand to a broader area. This is because a large number of displaced persons are using natural resources for their own supplies and business benefits. These issues have caused a lot of damage to the wildlife, which is losing habitat and being hunted. There are only a few wild animals found in the shelters areas, which indicate that deforestation has a major effect on the environment and ecosystem.

Reference

TBBC, 2010: *Burmese Border Refugee Sites with Population Figures*; at: http://www.tbbc.org/camps/2010-06-jun-map-tbbc-unhcr.pdf.

Masantia, Major Jirasak. (2000). Role of Western Non-Governmental Organizations in assisting the Karen refugees along the Thai-Myanmar Border, Political Science MA. Thesis, Chiangmai University, Chiangmai Province.

Vogler, Pia (2007). Into the Jungle of Bureaucracy: Negotiating Access to Camps at the Thai-Burma Border. Department of International Development, University of Oxford, United Kingdom. Refugee Survey Quarterly, Vol. 26, Issue 3 DOI:10.1093/rsq/hdi0242

Chapter 4
The Way of Living and Resource Utilisation of the Displaced People

Suwattana Thadaniti, Kanokphan U-Sha, Bart Lambregts, Jaturapat Bhiromkaew, Saowanee Wijitkosum, Vollop Prombang and Suchaow Toommakorn

Abstract The impact of the way of living of the displaced persons is described and illustrated, including long- and short-term effects. Bringing in such a large population in a relatively unplanned way, particularly when the issue was seen originally as temporary, has many unforeseen consequences and impacts in terms of erosion, pollution, unsustainable use of natural resources and competition with the local population. The latter has led to some tension and conflict. Where traditional and cultural ways of living have not been accommodated by the provision of humanitarian resources, for example types of cooking oil and food, the local environment has been utilised to supplement what is available. The result has been a range of negative environmental impacts.

Keywords Soil erosion · Waste disposal · Housing types · Garbage disposal · Garbage burning · Latrines · Water erosion · Environmental impact

---

S. Thadaniti (✉)
Social Research Institute, Chulalongkorn University, Bangkok, Thailand
e-mail: tsuwattana@yahoo.com

K. U-Sha
Institute of Asian Studies, Chulalongkorn University, Bangkok, Thailand

B. Lambregts
Division of Urban and Environmental Planning, Faculty of Architecture, Kasetsart University, Bangkok, Thailand

J. Bhiromkaew
Royal Thai Police, Bangkok, Thailand

S. Wijitkosum
Environmental Research Institute, Chulalongkorn University, Bangkok, Thailand

V. Prombang
Royal Thai survey department, Bangkok, Thailand

S. Toommakorn
Pisut Technology Consultant Company, Bangkok, Thailand

S. Thadaniti and S. Chantavanich (eds.), *The Impact of Displaced People's Temporary Shelters on Their Surrounding Environment*, SpringerBriefs in Environment, Security, Development and Peace 16, DOI: 10.1007/978-3-319-02842-2_4,

4.1 Introduction

The livelihood of displaced people in the temporary shelters has environmental impacts which, in turn, may affect local communities living nearby or downstream. Like other people, displaced persons use land, construct dwellings and utilities, use resources and produce and dispose of waste. Since the shelters are not easily allowed to expand, they are chronically overcrowded. The overcrowding of the shelters contributes to an environmental problem. It contributes to the rapid depletion of natural resources both inside and outside the shelters; it leads to overburdening of public utilities and facilities; and it aggravates waste disposal problems. Various kinds of pollution are often the result, affecting not only the displaced persons but also sometimes the local communities living nearby. These conditions basically apply to most if not all shelters, as they all come under the same directions of the Royal Thai Government (RTG) and the international humanitarian agencies. Hence, remedies for this problem require the involvement not only of the displaced person but also of those shaping the conditions in which displaced person live.

4.2 Land Use

4.2.1 Tham Hin

The Tham Hin temporary shelter is located on a steep slope. It is divided into an Office, a Household and Recreation Zones. The Office Zone is the public zone. Entrance to the Office Zone is by permission only. The Office Zone is located opposite of the temporary shelter's main street and next to the foothills. It is home to the UNHCR office, the school, the clinic, the International Rescue Committee (IRC) office and the community stores.

The Household Zone is the residential area in the temporary settlement. It is divided into three separated zones for easy management. Houses are mostly one or two storey and made of bamboo. Rattan is used to tie composing parts together. Each zone has a sports ground and a church, since most of the displaced person are Christian. Around their houses, the displaced persons are able to grow a few vegetables for family consumption. The recreation area is located near the entrance of the shelter, about two rai in size or 0.32 hec. It is a sport arena and meeting place mainly used by teenagers in the evening. It is also used by the vocational training centre.

Displaced persons use the land directly surrounding the shelter to grow crops and vegetables. This land is granted to the displaced persons by the Catholic Office for Emergency Relief and Refugees (COERR), which also provides vocational

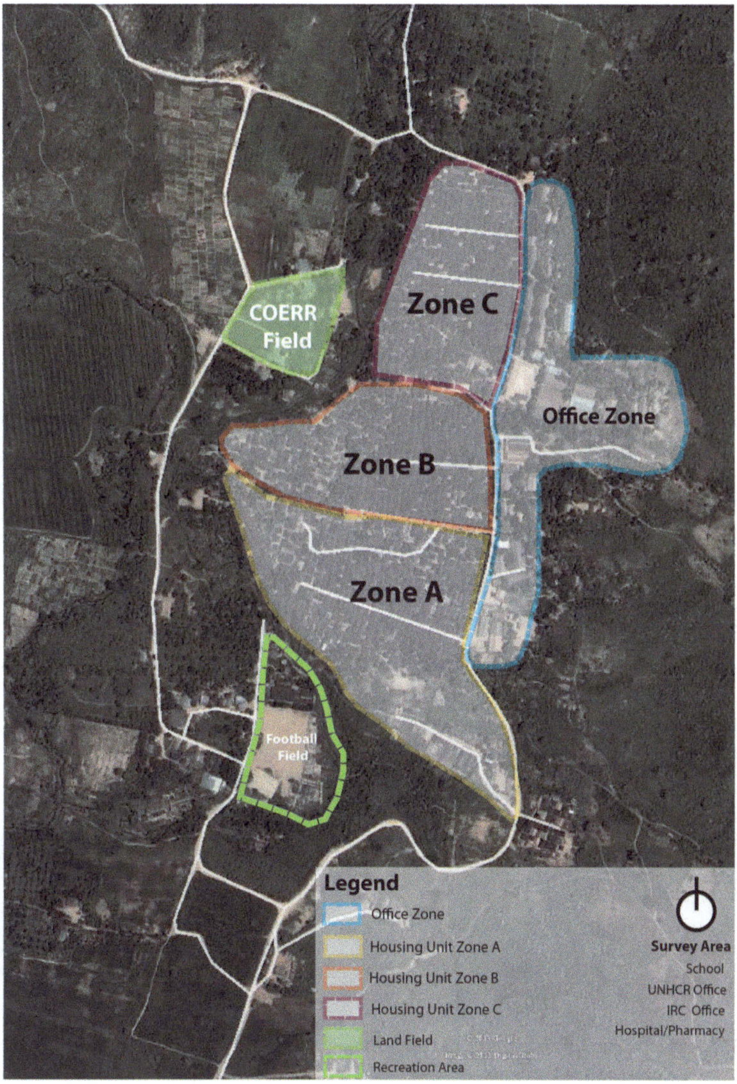

Fig. 4.1 Land zoning in Tham Hin Temporary Shelter. *Source* The Authors

training for the displaced person in an attempt to make their lives more productive in the temporary settlement. Among the crops grown are corn, sugar cane, rubber trees and various vegetables for daily consumption in the temporary settlement (Figs. 4.1, 4.2, 4.3, 4.4 and 4.5).

Fig. 4.2 Impression of central areas. *Source* Photos taken by study team

Fig. 4.3 Sports ground and a church in the residential area. *Source* Photo taken by study team

4.2.2 Ban Mai Nai Soi

In Ban Mai Nai Soi temporary shelter most land is used for residential purposes. Commercial functions are concentrated around the places where people are likely to gather or pass by frequently, such as the Moi Office, Pok 3, the clinic, Pok 14 and the EH centre in Pok 2. Most of the space in the recreation area is used as a football field, the school and other official spaces. Furthermore, there is a small cultivated area organised by COERR to facilitate household gardening for home consumption (Figs. 4.6, 4.7, 4.8, 4.9 and 4.10).

Fig. 4.4 Sports ground and a church in the residential area. *Source* Photo taken by study team

Fig. 4.5 Cultivated area outside the temporary settlement. *Source* Photo taken by study team

4.2.3 Mae La

Most of the land in Mae La temporary shelter is used for residential purposes. Office, commercial and recreational functions are dispersed across the shelter's different zones, with a concentration found along the main street of the C Zone. Vegetables and other edibles for home consumption are grown around the houses, as space permits. Beyond the shelter's boundaries, crops are grown in a larger

Fig. 4.6 Agricultural products available for sale inside the temporary settlement. *Source* Photo taken by study team

scale and also for commercial purposes. The land is rented from local Thai people (Figs. 4.11, 4.12 and 4.13).

4.3 Utilities and Facilities

4.3.1 Tham Hin

Water for consumption is stored at the top of a mountain above the temporary settlement. Water is pumped up there and kept in a water tank behind the IRC office. Water is distributed to the residents in the morning, afternoon and evening until 18.00 h, after which supply is cut off. Water is delivered to each residential zone every 4 h through a system of PVC pipes. Electricity is supplied by the Provincial Electricity Authority. Backup capacity is provided by a generator that serves certain units such as the temporary settlement office, the health care centre and the school. Households also rely on batteries, candles and kerosene lamps for lighting.

News and information is disseminated inside the temporary settlement via shelter broadcasts. Usually, it is in the form of announcement and communications circulated in the church and school.

Tham Hin is not only a temporary shelter for displaced person, it is also the coordination centre for government sectors and international agencies. Tham Hin also has two schools, staffed by camp staff. The educational system is divided into five levels: kindergarten, primary school level, middle school level, high school level and university level, the latter unofficial.

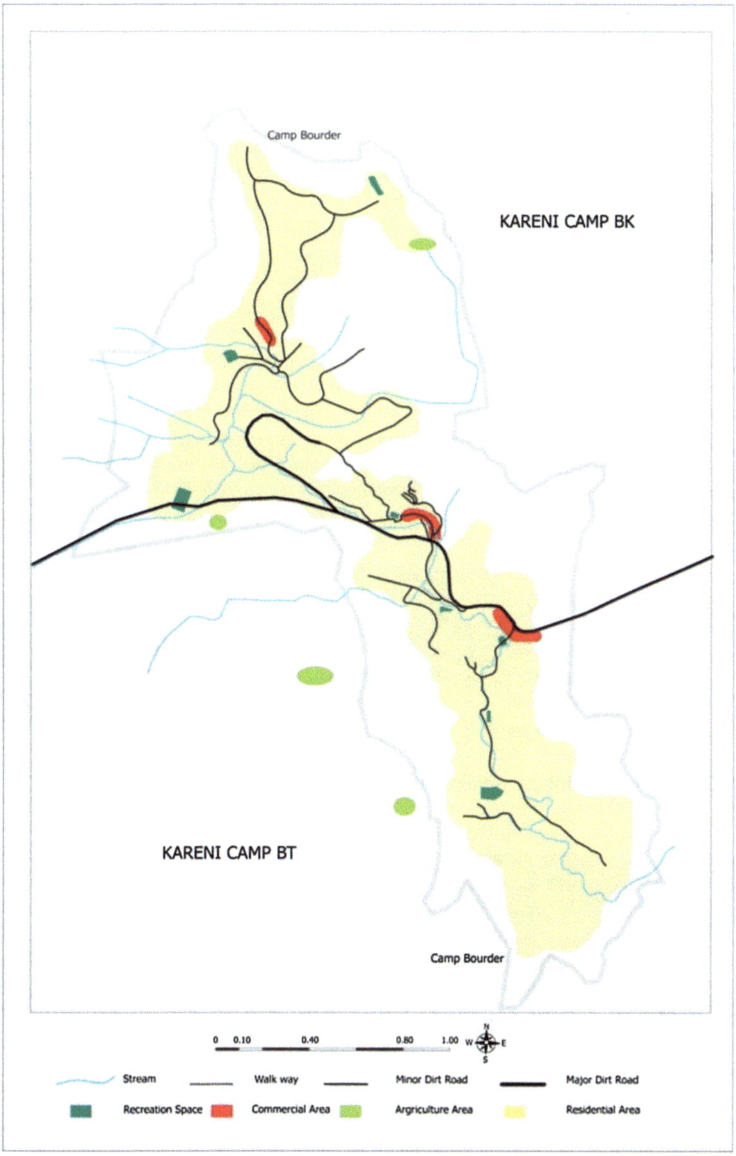

Fig. 4.7 Land use in Ban Mai Nai Soi Temporary Shelter. *Source* Obtained from a survey

As the result of space limitations, morning and afternoon classes are broken according to level of study. Kindergarten, primary school and middle school students study in the morning. Displaced people learn Karen, English and Thai language. High school and college students go to school in the afternoon. At the college level, classes are taught in English and the curriculum is managed by the ZOA.

Fig. 4.8 Residential buildings. *Source* Photo taken by study team

Fig. 4.9 Commercial buildings. *Source* Photo taken by study team

Fig. 4.10 Recreation area. *Source* Photo taken by study team

There is one hospital located in the UNHCR area. This hospital can admit up to 30 patients as long as they have common illnesses that can be treated with medicine. There is also a recovery room for male and female patients. If a patient has a severe illness, the Thai Volunteer Militia or *Or Sor* is asked for permission to send that patient to either Suanpueng hospital or Ratchaburi hospital, depending on the patient's symptoms.

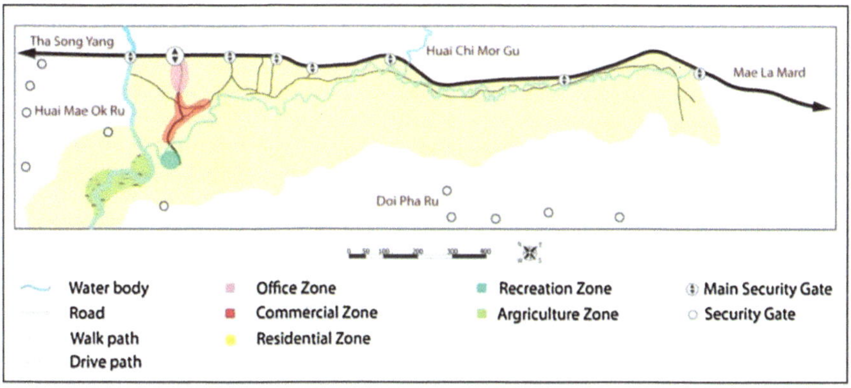

Fig. 4.11 Land use in Mae La Temporary Shelter. *Source* Derived from a survey

Fig. 4.12 Commercial buildings. *Source* Photo taken by study team

Fig. 4.13 Recreation area. *Source* Photo taken by study team

Most of the displaced person population is Christian; therefore, churches are located in every zone of the shelter. There are reportedly four churches, one mosque and one Buddhist temple (Figs. 4.14, 4.15, 4.16, 4.17 and 4.18).

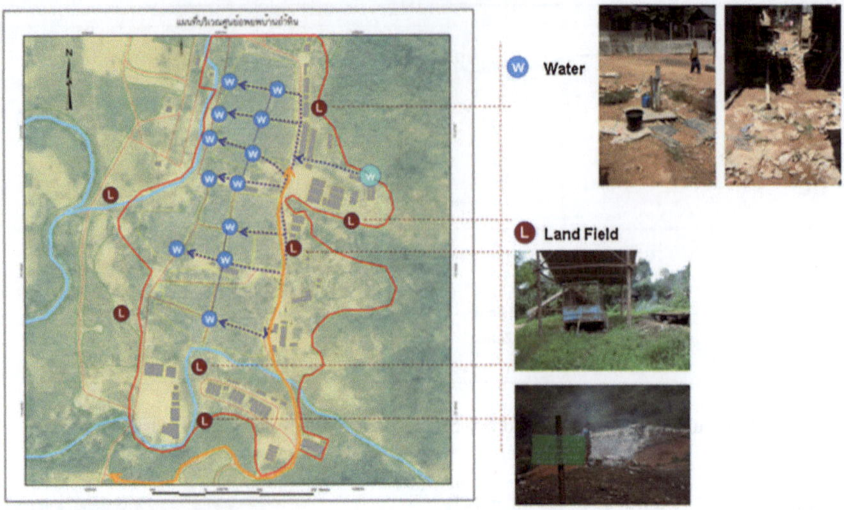

Fig. 4.14 Overview of public utilities in Tham Hin. *Source* The Authors

Fig. 4.15 Water distribution inside the temporary settlement. *Source* Photo taken by study team

Fig. 4.16 School buildings in Tham Hin. *Source* Photo taken by study team

Fig. 4.17 Hospital in Tham Hin. *Source* Photo taken by study team

Fig. 4.18 Church and a Buddhist religious place. *Source* Photo taken by study team

4.3.2 Ban Mai Nai Soi

Ban Mai Nai Soi temporary shelter has 2 medical centres and 23 schools. The latter include 6 kindergartens, 13 primary schools Grade 1–4, 5 primary schools grade G-8 and middle schools and 1 high school. As for religious places, the shelter counts nine Christian churches and one Buddhist temple. Water is obtained from the surrounding mountains (Figs. 4.19, 4.20, 4.21 and 4.22).

4.3.3 Mae La

The main source of water is the Pha Roo creek. Water is pumped up and stored in a water tank located on a high spot in the area. It is supplied to the residents in the morning and evening. In the shelter's southern part, water is obtained from Doi

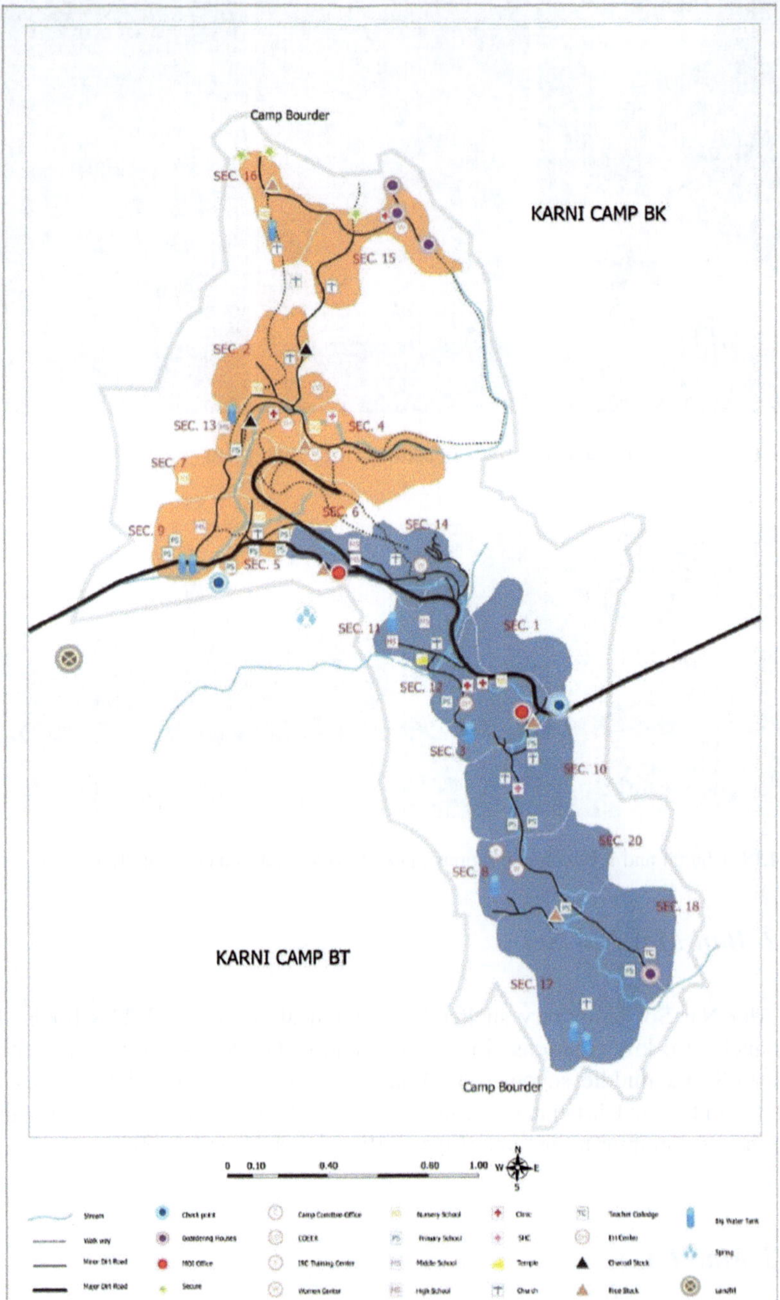

Fig. 4.19 Overview of utilities and facilities at Ban Mai Nai Soi. *Source* The Authors

Fig. 4.20 Office buildings. *Source* Photo taken by study team

Fig. 4.21 Hospital buildings. *Source* Photo taken by study team

Fig. 4.22 School building. *Source* Photo taken by study team

Lae Wah hill as well as from about 60 water wells dug in the vicinity of Chi Mor Ku creek.

Electrical power is transmitted from the Provincial Electricity Authority to certain places such as the temporary settlement office, hospital and school. Meanwhile, the residents use battery, candles and kerosene lamps as a source of

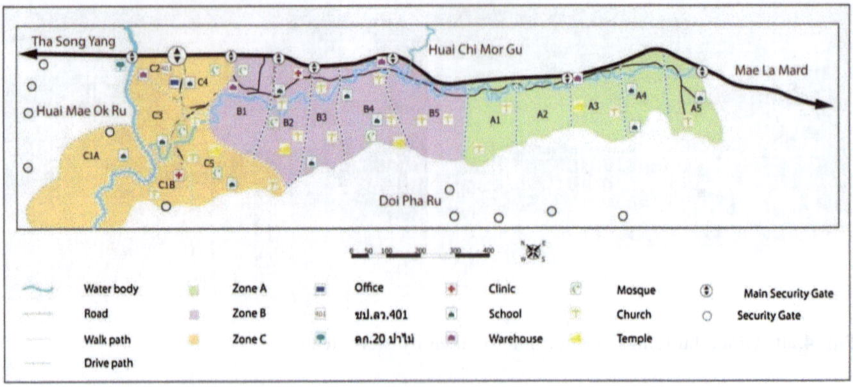

Fig. 4.23 Overview of utilities and facilities in Mae La. *Source* Department of the Interior

power. The shelter office is used as a broadcasting station from where news is disseminated. There are eight other spots where information is publicised. The office of the temporary shelter Mae La is a coordination centre for government sectors, international agencies and organisations and the displaced person committees.

Mae La has 18 kindergartens, 14 primary schools, 4 middle schools, 5 high schools and 1 special educational school. Four languages, Burmese, Karen, English and Thai, are used as a medium for instruction. There is one Thai language school run by a Thai Volunteer Militia member.

There are two medical centres: the General Medical Centre organised by AMI, and the Physical Disability Centre organised by HI. In addition to these there are three Malaria Prevention Research Units dispersed across the shelter. The Planned Parenthood Association of Thailand (PPAT) under the patronage of H.R.H. the Princess Mother, has a presence as well and focuses on family planning.

The shelter has four Buddhist temples and four mosques. Furthermore, there are 23 churches including 15 Protestant/Baptist, 6 SDA and 2 Anglican churches (Figs. 4.23, 4.24 and 4.25).

4.4 Housing and the Environment

4.4.1 Tham Hin

Dwellings in Tham Hin are mostly made of bamboo with the composite parts tied together with rattan or bamboo. Three types of houses can be distinguished: the one-storey bamboo house, the two-storey bamboo house and the one-storey raised floor bamboo house.

Fig. 4.24 The surrounding area of the office of the temporary shelter. *Source* Photo taken by study team

Fig. 4.25 School located in the temporary settlement. *Source* Photo taken by study team

Fig. 4.26 One-storey bamboo houses. *Source* Photo taken by study team

The one-storey bamboo house typically houses four to five persons, which is normally a family unit. This is a popular housing type. Since the shelter is built on steep slopes, the houses often have their floors raised above the ground by about 50 cm. Such raised floors create space underneath the houses where waste can be

Fig. 4.27 Two-storey bamboo houses. *Source* Photo taken by study team

discharged. Liquid waste is allowed to run off the sloping ground. The elevated floors also help to prevent wild animals to enter the houses in the rainy season. The survey also found that some well-to-do families use concrete floors for their house. Often such structures are then also used as stores (Fig. 4.26).

The two-storey bamboo house typically sleeps 5 to 10 persons. The use of materials and construction techniques are similar to the ones used for the one-storey buildings. Two-storey bamboo houses are mostly used for residential purposes, and occasionally for commercial purposes (Fig. 4.27).

The one-storey raised floor bamboo house provides a roof for four to five persons as well. Like the normal one-storey house, it is a popular housing style. The floor is raised about 1.5 m above the ground. This creates space for the storage

Fig. 4.28 One-storey raised floor bamboo house. *Source* Photo taken by study team

Fig. 4.29 Ground surface collapse/pollution from burning/housing density. *Source* Photo taken by study team

of for example equipment, building materials or charcoal. This type of house is often found in areas that are prone to flooding (Fig. 4.28).

The survey reveals that the living environment in the residential zones is rather poor. It is crowded, with the bamboo huts standing side by side along narrow alleyways. Waste and sewage are poorly managed, with households having no other choice than to let wastewater flow from their houses along the slopes freely, so causing the ground surface to deteriorate and heightening the risk of the soil to collapse. The inhabitants try to solve this problem by piling sandbags so as to prevent further soil erosion. However, this method has not been very successful. A related problem is that wastewater running down from the houses at higher elevations often creates puddles of wastewater underneath the houses located at lower levels.

Fig. 4.30 Puddle of wastewater/improved scenery/planting on leftover space. *Source* Photo taken by study team

Fig. 4.31 Cooking pollution/improved scenery. *Source* Photo taken by study team

Since the houses are built so close to each other, with often only a metre of space between them, problems of smell and smoke are inevitable. Bad smells from toilets and smoke from cooking are usually noticeable throughout the neighbourhoods.

Attempts to improve the living environment in the residential zones are being made. The displaced persons not only try to use whatever space is left between the dwellings to grow vegetables and other types of vegetation for the purpose of consumption but also to make the area look nicer (Figs. 4.29, 4.30 and 4.31).

The survey found that most materials used to build the dwellings last for about 2 years, depending on the construction technique and maintenance. Some houses have been destroyed by Dinoderus Minutus, a bamboo pest. For a new house, the

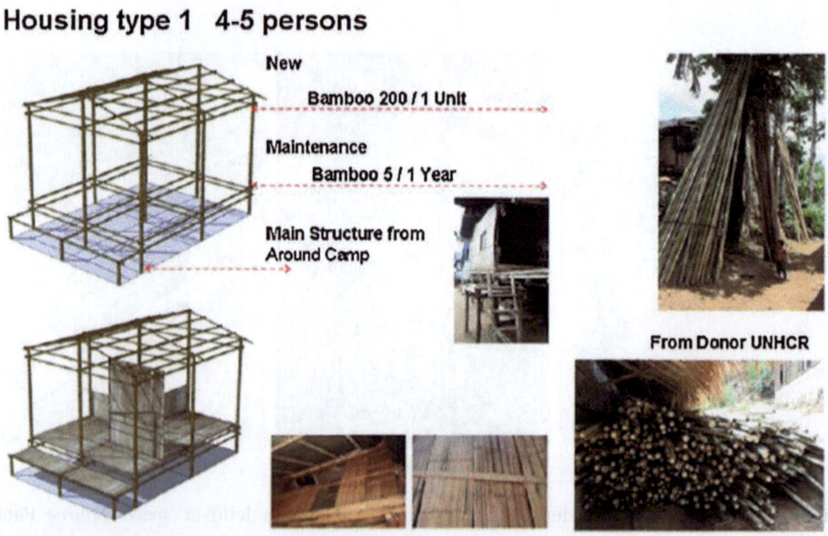

Fig. 4.32 Construction of a one-storey bamboo house. *Source* Photo taken by study team

Fig. 4.33 Building materials and housing structure. *Source* Photo taken by study team

TBBC provides about 200 pieces of bamboo. On top of that it supplies five pieces per year for maintenance. Bamboo poles are used to build the major parts of the house such as the structure, ceiling joists and the roof. Hardwood such as Eucalyptus wood and redwood is used to build the stilts that support the house; two-storey houses occasionally also use concrete stilts for support. Nowadays, redwood is rare, and Eucalyptus wood is used instead. Rooves nowadays are made of canvas. Canvas lasts about 5 years, whereas the dried-leaf of cogon grass that was used previously remains good for only 2 years. Currently, cogon grass is hard to find as an investor has transformed the area surrounding the temporary settlement into a rubber plantation. Sometimes, in case they cannot wait any longer for donated wood to arrive, the displaced person look for lumber in the forest surrounding the temporary settlement (Fig. 4.32).

4.4.2 Ban Mai Nai Soi

Most of the dwellings in the shelter are raised floor houses that have their composing parts tied together with rattan or bamboo. The raised floors help to prevent flooding during the rainy season. The houses vary in size, depending on the number of family members. The common size is about 4 by 5 m. The dwellings are built mostly of bamboo, while eucalyptus wood is used for the stilts and dried Tong Tueng leaves are used for roofing. The TBBC supplies the building materials, also for maintenance (Fig. 4.33).

Fig. 4.34 One-storey/two-storey house/two-storey raised floor houses. *Source* Photo taken by study team

Fig. 4.35 Growing vegetables and keeping pigs around the house. *Source* Photo taken by study team

4.4.3 Mae La

Bamboo is also the construction material of choice in Mae La. The composing parts of the dwellings are tied together with rattan or bamboo. There are three types of houses: one-storey houses, two-storey houses and two-storey raised floor houses. The one-storey houses are mostly located on the main street of the shelter. Generally, the one-storey houses are used to run a business such as a grocery store, saloon or convenience store. The two-storey houses are located everywhere in the shelter. These are residential houses with a clear division of functional spaces.

Fig. 4.36 Space underneath the house/containers storing water obtained from rain. *Source* Photo taken by study team

Fig. 4.37 Dried leaf for roofing, and bamboo used for walls, floors and house structure. *Source* Photo taken by study team

Bedroom space and space for general usage are found on the second floor, while the kitchen and storage room for firewood, charcoal or maintenance materials are found downstairs. The two-storey raised floor houses are mostly found in the higher areas of the shelter. Again, downstairs is for storage and cooking while upstairs is for general usage and sleeping. The floor space under the house helps to prevent water from flowing into the house in the rainy season (Fig. 4.34).

The yards around the house are used for gardening, growing vegetables and keeping such animals as chicken and pigs (Figs. 4.35 and 4.36).

TBBC supplies most of the materials needed for house construction and yearly maintenance. The donated materials include bamboo, which is used for floors, walls, stilts, ceiling joists and other building parts; Eucalyptus wood, which is used for stilt; and dried Tong Tueng leaves, which are used for roofing. Supplies, however, do not always meet demand, encouraging displaced person to sometimes search for building materials outside the shelter. Here they are able to also find hardwood such as red wood which is useful for stilts and other structural elements of their houses. However, the same materials are also needed by Karen–Thai who live in the area as well, and the increasing scarcity of these resources is becoming an issue between Karen–Thai and the displaced persons (Fig. 4.37).

4.5 Household Sewerage and Waste

4.5.1 Tham Hin

The survey shows that the sanitary system in the temporary settlement is far from healthy. Depending on the house types, latrines are built inside or outside the house. The latrine system is a squat toilet with a natural septic hole that has the capacity to hold sewage for 2–3 years, depending on the number of family member. However, since the temporary settlement is located on steep slopes and the building density is high, IRC has difficulties to manage the household sewerage properly. As a result, displaced persons face the problem of faecal sewage overflow and they have to dig new holes around their houses frequently. If nothing changes, space for digging new holes will soon become hard to find and it will

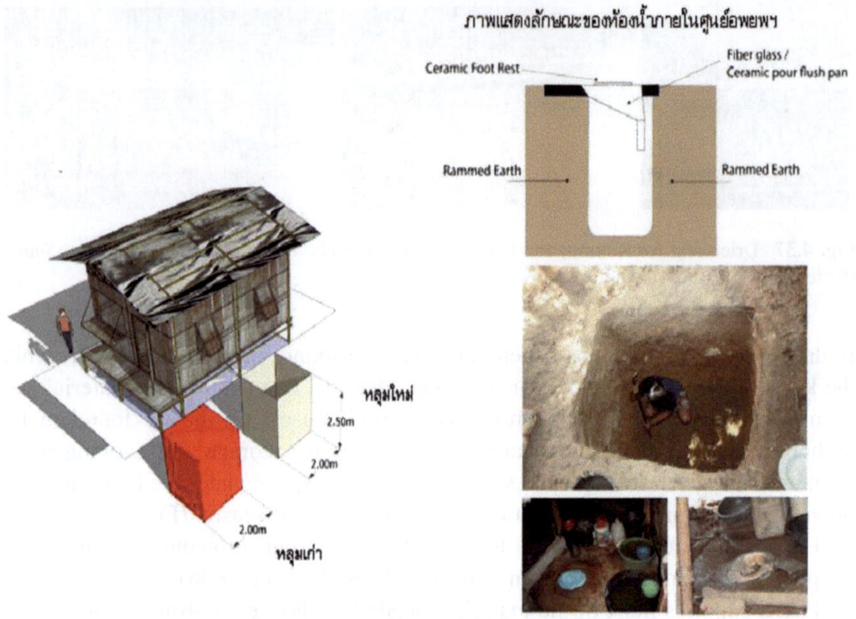

Fig. 4.38 Latrine system with natural cesspit. *Source* The Authors

become even more difficult to maintain hygiene (information received from an interview) (Fig. 4.38).

The walls of the cesspit are uncovered because cement pipes, which are actually offered for sale by the IRC, are considered too expensive or at least unaffordable by the displaced persons. As a result, sewage continuously seeps into the surrounding soil, causing an environmental impact and a health hazard to the displaced persons.

The shelter inhabitants dispose of their wastewater basically in two ways. The first is by digging holes using layers of stones as filters and letting the filtered wastewater slowly seep into the ground. The disadvantage of this method is that it attracts rats in search of food during the night time. The rats in turn may carry diseases that once passed on to humans may spread quickly among the shelter population. The second and most commonly practiced way is by simply letting the wastewater run off the slopes. It has the same disadvantage as the former method and on top of that causes damage to the ground surface. Both methods, directly and indirectly, cause wastewater to end up in the same creek that is also used for water supply, which is obviously not a very healthy situation.

IRC is responsible for garbage management. It has distributed garbage cans across the shelter which are emptied every other day. Garbage is then brought to one of seven garbage disposal stations. The disposal method used is landfill. A disposal station normally consists of two big holes located next to each other. One is for wet garbage while the other hole is used to incinerate dry garbage. A very

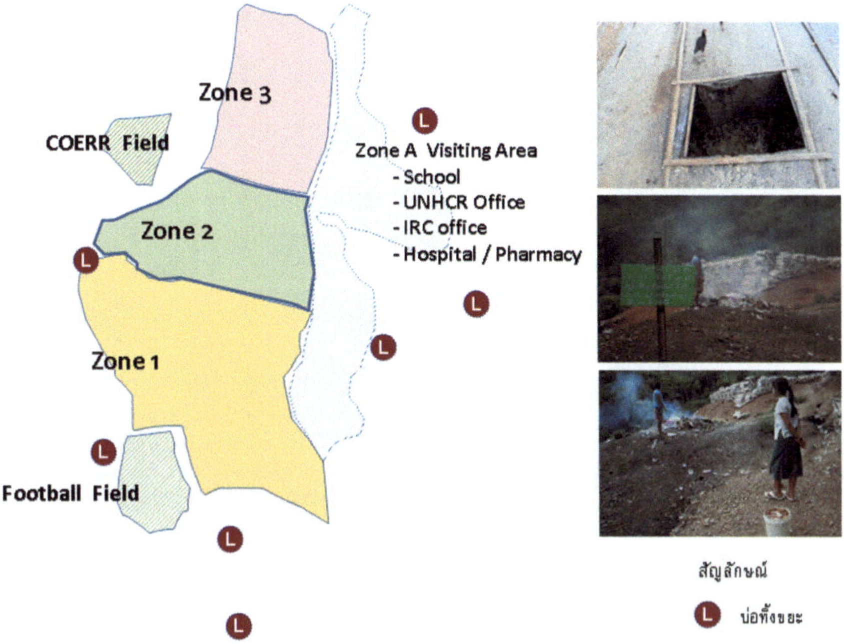

Fig. 4.39 Garbage disposal sites in Tham Hin. *Source* The Authors

likely future problem is lack of space to dig new holes to dispose of the increasing amount of garbage generated by the shelter population (Figs. 4.39 and 4.40).

4.5.2 Ban Mai Nai Soi

In Ban Mai Nai Soi the IRC has developed two latrine systems. The first uses a concrete tank and the second a 3-m deep natural septic hole or cesspit where sewage is allowed to infiltrate into the ground. The first model is used in the health care centre. The second model is commonly used by the displaced persons.

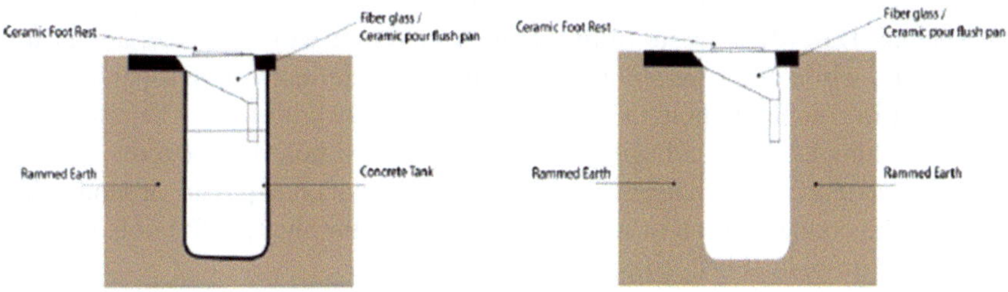

Fig. 4.40 Disposal sites around the temporary settlement. *Source* Photo taken by study team

IRC is also responsible for household wastewater management. Houses are provided with a zinc trough that holds wastewater from cooking and other activities and directs it to open sewage channels running in front of the houses. These channels guide the wastewater to the lowest areas in the shelter area (Fig. 4.41).

IRC encourages every household to keep their garbage in a fertiliser sack and to bring these to one of the 30 garbage collection stations. From Monday to Friday, the garbage truck will pick up garbage from these stations and bring it to the disposal site. Hazardous waste from the medical centre will be incinerated at the disposal site, while other hazardous waste such as batteries will be separated and disposed of in a concrete hole that can be closed tightly with a lid. The remaining garbage is dumped in a garbage hole or landfill. The hole has concrete paving around but no canvas or whatsoever underneath. The concrete paving around helps to prevent the contamination of water sources around the shelter. The hole is 25 m deep and 30 m wide (Figs. 4.42 and 4.43).

Fig. 4.41 Household water disposal/zinc trough holding wastewater/wastewater channels. *Source* Photo taken by study team

Fig. 4.42 'Natural' waste disposal hole. *Source* Photo taken by study team

Fig. 4.43 Concrete hole for hazardous waste/incinerator for hazardous waste. *Source* Photo taken by study team

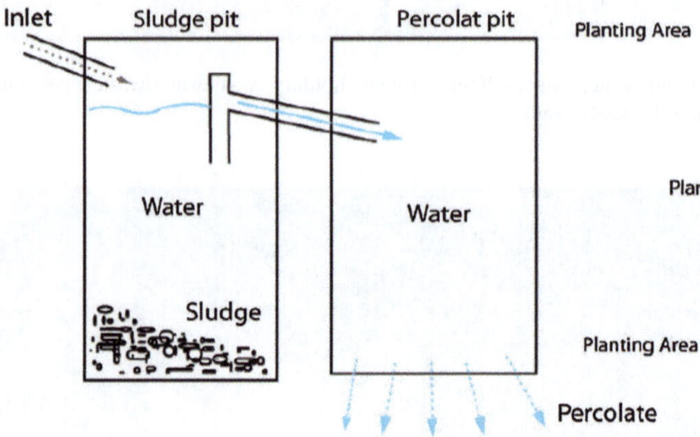

Fig. 4.44 Two-pit latrine system. *Source* Photo taken by study team

4.5.3 Mae La

In Mae La the bathroom and latrine are mostly built outside the house, at the back. Solidarities are responsible for bathroom and latrine management. Latrines have a sludge and a percolation pit to prolong waste disposal pickup time. This type of latrine is commonly used in the healthcare centre, office and in most of the

Fig. 4.45 Wastewater from cooking and from livestock. *Source* Photo taken by study team

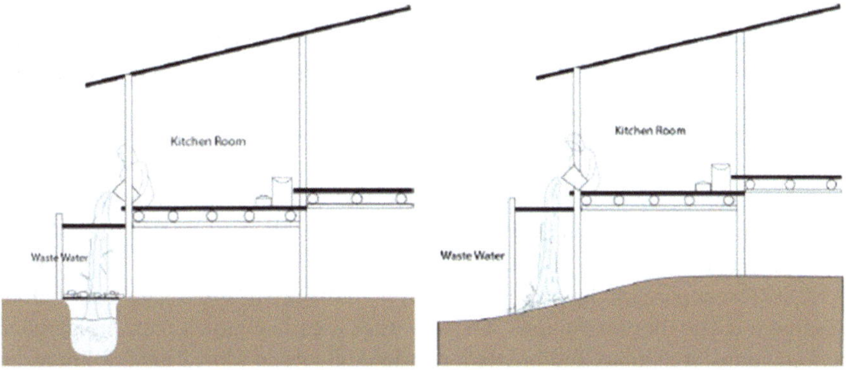

Fig. 4.46 Wastewater retained in a hole/allowed to run off. *Source* Photo taken by study team

displaced persons' houses. However, from the survey it also emerged that some houses still use natural septic holes. This mostly concerns houses where illegal displaced person live, as Solidarities do not provide assistance to them (Fig. 4.44).

Fig. 4.47 Transfer stations. *Source* Photo taken by study team

Fig. 4.48 Disposal site. *Source* Photo taken by study team

Solidarities encourage households to dig a hole to retain their wastewater from cooking. However, the survey discloses that some households, especially those living in the higher areas of the shelter, do not comply and let their wastewater run off the slopes and infiltrate the ground. Wastewater from laundry and from raising livestock is not retained or otherwise managed. In result, part of this wastewater seeps freely into the ground, while another part flows into Chi Mo Ku creek and Mae Oak Hu creek. Both creeks are also used for water supply: Chi Mo Ku creek provides water for the shelter population, Mae Oak Hu is a source of water for both the shelter population and for local communities living outside the shelter (Figs. 4.45 and 4.46).

COERR encourages households to keep garbage in a garbage can before bringing it to the transfer stations. Twice a week a garbage truck picks up garbage from the transfer stations and brings it to a landfill site in Moo 2 area, 7 km away from the shelter (Figs. 4.47 and 4.48).

4.6 Environmental Impacts Within the Displaced Persons' Temporary Settlement

4.6.1 Ban Tam Hin

4.6.1.1 Aquatic Environment

The general topography at the temporary shelter for displaced people is forests, surrounded with valley and a mountain called Hub Ka Torn. The creek flowing through the southern area of the shelter is named Huai Nam Khun. The water supply system is available here for consumption. The raw water is pumped from subterranean course of water from the mountain. The water consumption is limited for using at 25 l per person a day.

Fig. 4.49 Lavatory with septic tank in the shelter of evacuee. *Source* Photo taken by study team

Fig. 4.50 Wastewater course caused by the direct pouring of wastewater. *Source* Photo taken by study team

Impacts from Sanitary and Wastewater Conditions

According to the displaced persons' habit in using water and the toilets which do not have proper sanitary wastewater, the toilet there is like a lavatory with septic tank drilled into the soil, and put the toilet sump above. Sewage will be absorbed in the soil, with contamination effects to groundwater which will then flow to the river and canal. Throwing wastewater directly into the soil leads to some of water permeating the soil to mix with groundwater before flowing to the river. The rest of the wastewater will erode the ground and cause wastewatercourse. The wastewatercourse is blocked for long periods of time and is the source of diseases including from animals. It impacts on health and causes bad smells in the surrounding area. The main problems arising from the displaced person' behaviour, pouring wastewater directly to the soil, is to wash the ground soil away.

Fig. 4.51 Soil erosion caused by directly pouring wastewater. *Source* Photo taken by study team

The displaced persons try to solve the problem of soil erosion by placing fertiliser bags on the ground soil, but it cannot reduce the impact (Figs. 4.49, 4.50 and 4.51).

The wastewater's impact in the shelter is not only from dumping wastewater, but also due to the lack of good management such as leachate from landfill near the water source. This can be seen in garbage dump and waste-burnt zones at Ban Tham Hin shelters, which lack waste management and garbage disposal systems. The displaced persons throw and burn garbage and trash along the creek area. When it rains, the rain will wash the dirt and germs from the garbage dumps or from such heaps of waste to the water sources. In addition, the waste side holes are not placed by plastic or waterproof materials. Normally, the garbage landfill should have natural clay with its thickness at least 5 m to support the water-resistant material layer (Department of Groundwater Resources, 2006) in order to prevent leakage and contamination from garbage such as germs, bacteria, metal substances and many more to flow into the underground water and soil in the surrounding areas. Waste-contaminated water causes big impacts to the quality of

Fig. 4.52 Garbage dump and garbage-burnt zones, along the creek area. *Source* Photo taken by study team

Fig. 4.53 The steep location. *Source* Photo taken by study team

Fig. 4.54 The Creek in the evacuation area. *Source* Photo taken by study team

soil, underground water and ground water. Parts of underground water and ground water flow down into the water source rendering the dirtiness to the creek and also deteriorate water quality (Fig. 4.52).

The water utilisation of 8,711 displaced persons (TBBC 2010) can approximate in the amount of wastewater at 80 % of the total amount of water used. The refugee of water utilisation is approximately 174,220 l/day.

Ban Tham Hin is located in the steep hill area with Huai Nam Khun flowing through the lower part of the shelter. The wastewater from daily basis use, involving the wastewater flown by rain, causes piles of sediments to the lowland, Huai Nam Khun, It causes dirt and germs, affecting to the quality of water at Huai

Fig. 4.55 The area for burning garbage. *Source* Photo taken by study team

Nam Khun. From the survey, we find that some part of the creek is clear, but some is opaque in brown colour, which may cause from the blow of sediment in the refugee shelter area, resulting opaque water colour. The soil erosion is caused by dumping wastewater directly to the soil, which is the main problem found in Ban Tham Hin shelter (Figs. 4.53 and 4.54).

Impacts from the Garbage Disposal System

Two methods of garbage disposal are used. First, eliminate by disposing of garbage in the hole. The garbage which is thrown here is wet garbage. When the hole is full, the garbage will be buried and then fill the garbage pit. Second, incineration. This way is used for dry waste. The garbage hole and garbage incineration are in the same area around the shelter zone. The garbage holes do not use waterproof materials, which would help in preventing contamination of impurities into the soil and underground water. Department of Groundwater Resources (2006) considered the impact to the environment of constructing garbage landfill by observing suitable areas for constructing garbage landfill and classifying selection criteria such as being located at least 700 m away from water wells for consumption and water manufacturing and not in the community area.

In a comparison between garbage landfill used at Ban Tham Hin and selection criteria drawn up by Department of Groundwater Resources, we notice that there are several landfill sites located near the natural water sources incompatible to the criteria, especially that which states the garbage landfill area should be located away from natural or man-made water sources, including wetland at least 300 m since it can cause dirt contamination to the groundwater source. However, there is no information in selecting area for constructing garbage landfill of evacuee, so we cannot compare with other criteria.

A consequence of having the waste dump around the shelter is that the area becomes the breeding place for disease, and people will suffer from air pollution of the waste odour from garbage and smoke from garbage burning. The research also indicates that the garbage may be blown by the wind and rain and contaminate the water resources near the area, which affects water quality and the outer areas (Fig. 4.55).

Fig. 4.56 Subterranean course area and water caused by subterranean course. *Source* Photo taken by study team

4.6.2 Ban Mai Nai Soi

4.6.2.1 Aquatic Environment

The temporary shelter for displaced people at Ban Mai Nai Soi is located in the national reserved forest area, Mar Pai lower right side forest, watershed class 1 A, which is abundant with trees and also be the origin of water resource. The topography of the temporary shelter for displaced people is forest consisting of two parts, Ban Pang Kwai and Ban Pang Tractor. The water supply sources for consumption consist of subterranean courses and from wells.

A subterranean course is found five points in the forest shelter area. There are in Pok 9, 10, 11, 13, 16 and 19. The subterranean course at Pok 11 provides the water in the most quantity, sufficient for the refugee in Ban Pang Tractor. The water originating from the subterranean course will flow down, with a concrete barrier, through the installed pipe for distribution. This has a sieve to trap waste leaves that fall into the pipe. From the observation of physical basis of water quality, we found that the water is clear, not contaminated by waste or adulterated things which can be seen by eyes. There are not any activities performing in the surrounding area of subterranean course, so the water which flows from the subterranean course to the stream has a good quality, with no contaminated substances (Fig. 4.56).

A water well has been dug for storing water to use during the dry season. The size of the pond is 5 × 8 × 25 m, located in the Pok 13 forest area. The water from the well will be pumped up for water supply. In terms of water well quality, we found that water is clear, no contaminated substances such as leaves, garbage or other materials.

Water from the subterranean course and water well will be in water supply system, by flowing to the reservoir which is constructed by cement to an approximate size of 10 × 12 × 3 m. The water in the reservoir will be purified by chlorine to kill germs and be monitored for quality by IRC, in order to provide

Fig. 4.57 A water well which was dug for use during the dry season. *Source* Photo taken by study team

Fig. 4.58 A water quality treatment system, with reservoir for water treatment before distributing to refugee in each spot, and chlorine tank. *Source* Photo taken by study team

Fig. 4.59 The water supply source for distributing to be used in household: water tank; public space to get water and also shower place for women. *Source* Photo taken by study team

Fig. 4.60 Wastewater caused by the activities draining to the ground. *Source* Photo taken by study team

good quality of water to denizens for conversion. Water from the reservoir will flow to the water supply system and be distributed to various spots, at least one point per Pok such as a school, missionary school or clinic, for using in the household. The survey finds that some homes install the water supply system directly to their home for personal use (Figs. 4.57 and 4.58).

Impacts from Sanitary and Wastewater Conditions

Water distribution points for households were typically found in open space, with only one tap coming from the mountains for distributing to denizens or to cement wells with diameter 1.2 m. Each point can supply approximately 2,500 l of water. The space for utilising water in households is shared with the shower space divided by zinc. There are also other activities such as washing and cleaning carried out in this area without classifying the specific area to do each activity. There is no wastewater drainage system or pipe system, so the wastewater used in such activities flows to the ground and absorb directly to the soil (Figs. 4.59 and 4.60).

According to the research on household wastewater emission, denizens release wastewater from the kitchen directly to the ground passing through zinc gutters.

Fig. 4.61 Drainage system from the household: drainage gutter from kitchen and drainage from female toilet. *Source* Photo taken by study team

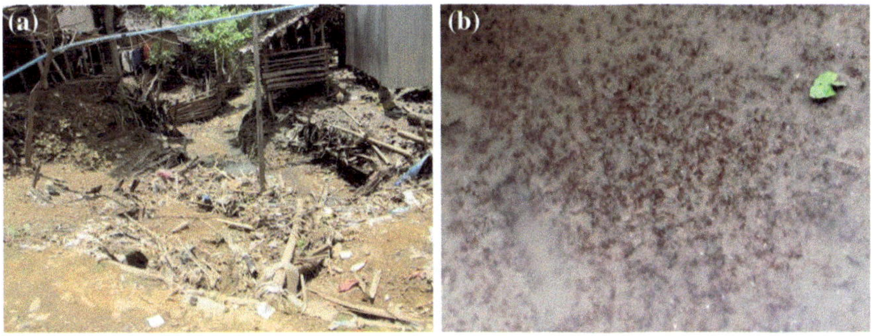

Fig. 4.62 The sewage watercourse leads to the accumulation of waste and becomes the breeding places of germs: watercourse leads to the accumulation of waste; and insects' embryos breed in blocked wastewater course. *Source* Photo taken by study team

This includes the wastewater from the toilet. As the time passes, the sewage watercourse will occur in the neighbourhood which leads to the accumulation of waste and becomes the breeding places of germs, bugs and carriers. Most of the household lavatories are cesspools or lavatories with septic tanks which is the cause of wastewater leakage to the ground. If the lavatory is located near water resources, the wastewater will contaminate the stream and ground water with Coliform bacteria or the bacteria that originate from the waste of the denizens (Figs. 4.61 and 4.62).

Wastewater generated from temporary shelter can be estimated at approximately 80 % of the overall water used; and the amount of water used 771,550 l/day, giving a figure for wastewater generated from denizens of 617,240 l/day.

The characteristics of shelters located in the reserved forest area and steep mountain render wastewater to flow downwards. The shelter area is also situated in the watershed area 1 A causing this area to be the origin of river flowing to meet with Pai River. In addition, Ban Mai Nai Soi shelter area has many streams flowing through, so the contaminated water will easily flow to the river. It shows that there are houses settled down near the water source and also use the stream as the transporting way. Therefore, the water is contaminated by waste and dirt easily and quickly.

From an observation of physical water sources, we find that the water source is a small stream, distributing to other areas. In some areas, water flows all the time, and is a muddy colour because the stream ground is mud and the water from other areas flowing down brings dust and sediment. The sediment in the stream which is used for transportation will be stirred by cars or people travelling back and forth. However, in some areas, we find that the water is clear due to the stream ground being stone or pebble. Therefore, the sediment is less than the muddy stream. From the survey, we find that there is garbage in every stream, contributing to the contaminated water sources with dirt and germ, especially if it is organic waste (Figs. 4.63, 4.64 and 4.65).

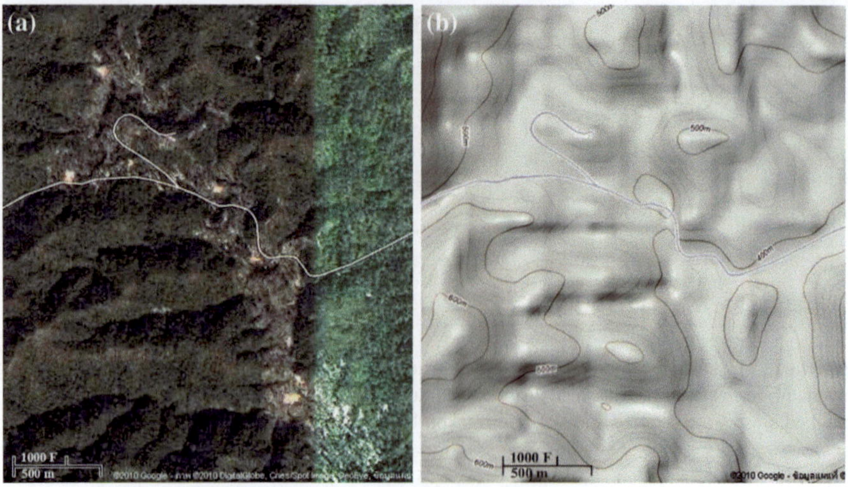

Fig. 4.63 Physical characteristic of the shelter for displaced people: shelters are settled in the national reserved forest, Mae Pai in lower right side; and the slope characteristic of the settlement area. *Source* Photo taken by study team

Fig. 4.64 Water resources and waterways at the shelter area. *Source* Photo taken by study team

Impacts from the Garbage Disposal System

From the survey and interviewing IRC staff, the agency which is responsible for waste disposal in the shelter area, we find that denizens eliminate garbage by putting them in the containers such as plastic and fertiliser bags and placing them at the provided space. IRC will keep them and bring to the garbage pit. However, we also find that some denizens do not throw garbage at the provided space. The garbage was found scattered in the residential areas, roads or water resources that

Fig. 4.65 Water resource and nearby houses: health centre is located near water resource; water resource used for transportation. *Source* Photo taken by study team

Fig. 4.66 Garbage scattered on the ground. *Source* Photo taken by study team

Fig. 4.67 Garbage pit nearby the mountain groove and waterway. *Source* Photo taken by study team

may be caused by the wind and rain leaching waste into the water, or directly throwing garbage into the water resources.

Pit landfills are found on the hill with groove and water flow down, where IRC has constructed a concrete container approximately 5 m in height for preventing garbage flowing down the hill. In the past, there was no flash flood flowing garbage down the hill. However, there is no garbage pit covered with plastic sheets for preventing infiltration of water into the ground rendering wastewater including rain leaching waste with dirt, and germs are absorbed into the ground and then flow to the water resources. This is one reason that affects the quality of the natural water resources.

The quantity of the garbage dump is approximately 1,000 kg weekly. It is a huge amount; consequently, garbage is left in the garbage pit. The gases from the garbage fermentation cause air pollution to the neighbouring area. Furthermore, the garbage pit is the breeding of bacteria that could spread to the shelter area. We find many flies in the garbage pit (Figs. 4.66 and 4.67).

4.6.3 Ban Mae La

The study of environmental impacts that results from displaced people who live in Ban Mae La temporary shelter shows the effects caused by behaviour and activities of displaced people by studying the links between the shelter area and surrounding environment. We collected primary data by observing, asking and interviewing displaced people in the shelter camp including the relevant authorities, and secondary data from various sources both from central and local government in major. Sample collection and laboratory experiments on water quality cannot be done due to the restriction in many areas.

Fig. 4.68 Subterranean course in the shelter area, zone C: subterranean course in the shelter area; and water quality from water supply system. *Source* Photo taken by study team

Fig. 4.69 Water supply system in the mountain: water tanks which are purified by chlorine; and tap for generating water to denizens. *Source* Photo taken by study team

4.6.3.1 Aquatic Environment

Ban Mae La is located in the Tha Song Yang national reserved forest with lots of mountains on the slope area. The temporary shelter is located in the second and third floor watersheds. Water quality index at the second floor watershed meet the specified watershed's quality. This area is suitable for being the upstream in the secondary order after the first floor watershed. In this watershed area, there is mining and planting perennial trees (Faculty of Liberal Arts Thammas at University, 1998). The water resources which are used in the shelter area come from natural water resource in the central area and nearby.

From the officer inquiry, we find that there are two subterranean watercourses in the mountain shelter area, zone A and zone C, which use the mentioned subterranean courses for distributing to denizens by a water supply system in the mountain. Water from the subterranean course is quite good in quality; the water is clear because the flowing path of water from subterranean course to water supply system in mountain passes through the forest, without agricultural activities and

Fig. 4.70 Ponds near the creek which were dug by villagers. *Source* Photo taken by study team

Fig. 4.71 Ground water pump. *Source* Photo taken by study team

community. The water is purified by chlorine before distributing to denizens (data from the interview) (Figs. 4.68 and 4.69).

Apart from the two subterranean courses in zone A and zone C, there are two more natural water resources where are used for consumption, Par Roo creek and Shi Mor Ku creek. Mae Ork Hu creek flows through some parts of the shelter area zone C, the upstream comes from the forest area, Moo 12, Ban Mae La Kee village and passes through the Ban Pa Lor Tee Kee Ta village to the shelter area. Water in the shelter area is pumped from the Par Roo creek, the pumped water being purified by chlorine to kill germs. The water in the creek is available for pumping only from June to February. From March to May, it is dry season; there is no water in Mae Ork Hu creek.

Shi Mor Ku creek flows through the shelter area. The upstream comes from forest near to shelter to meet with Huai Pa Toei and the subterranean course that flows from the shelter area to the creek. Shi Mor Ku creek flows through the shelter area from zone A to zone C. Denizens who use water from the Shi Mor Ku creek dig shallow wells near the creek to let the water leak to into the wells and use a dipper when they want to use water (Fig. 4.70).

In addition, ground water wells in the shelter area are dug by villagers. The space where the villagers use for pumping water is usually in the open space area. The villagers will use a water pump, lever or piston, to pump water for consumption. Water wells in the shelter area are also dug by the villagers themselves

Fig. 4.72 The water consumption activities in open areas. *Source* Photo taken by study team

Fig. 4.73 Waterway caused by water consumption without channel for Drainage. *Source* Photo taken by study team

Fig. 4.74 Wastewaterway accumulated and pollute to the environment. *Source* Photo taken by study team

(data from the interview). In the shelter area, there are three water wells available in zones A, B and C (Fig. 4.71).

Impacts from Sanitary and Wastewater Conditions

Wastewater quality was studied by water resource survey, physical characteristic of water resource, water consumption behaviour, disposal of wasted water and the pattern of housing and the denizens' toilet, including information obtained from interviews of the denizens and community leaders.

The area is mainly open without a channel for drainage. Therefore, the used water flows directly into the soil; some will seep in the area while some will flow to the surrounding area causing the flood tide waterway. The water may contaminate areas outside the shelter and natural water resource, especially during rain. Moreover, water consumption in the houses also has an influence on the water quality. The houses with a washing area are the open when the water is used for cooking or washing. The used water would flow directly into the soil without a channel for drainage. When the wastewater is regularly run, the waterway in the surrounding area would appear and cause an accumulation of the waste which comes with water such as food waste, garbage causing the foul odour pollution to the surrounding area and passers-by (Figs. 4.72, 4.73 and 4.74).

Furthermore, the characteristic of toilets in the denizens' household normally has the drainage into the ground near the toilets and the toilets mostly hold

Fig. 4.75 Domestic animals found in evacuation areas. *Source* Photo taken by study team

Fig. 4.76 Water quality examine in certain factors; and physical characteristic of water in Shi Mor Ku creek. *Source* Photo taken by study team

cesspools. To build the cesspool is by digging the ground and constructing a plaster above to create the cesspool without using concrete in the hole. That makes water from sewage absorb easily into the ground. If the toilets are located near the natural water sources, the wasted water can absorb and contaminate to the creek and ground water. Moreover, this can cause water from the creek and ground water to be contaminated by Coliform bacteria or diseases from excretion. The amount of wastewater in the temporary shelter is approximately 1,855,680 l/day.

Animal husbandry activities such as, pork, goat, dog and poultry rearing in the areas surround the denizens' house are sources of pathogens from animal waste.

Fig. 4.77 The denizens' habitation on the steep area. *Source* Photo taken by study team

Leaching from water and rain causes waste to be leached into the natural water sources in the area nearby (Fig. 4.75).

The physical water quality survey of the Shi Mor Ku creek was inspected on 2 September 2010, in the rainy season. The measurements of water quality in some factors found that PH values were equal to 7.49. Conductivity equal to 631 μs and temperature was 25.5 °C. The water looked cloudy brown with a very strong flow because of heavy rain. Large amounts of landfill waste were found in the water source (Fig. 4.76).

The activities and water consumption behaviour, plus the characteristics and location of the denizens' habitation on the steep hill, means wastewater from the activities done in the steep areas flows to the lower ground by gravity. Considering the nature of the natural water flow, it might flow into Shi Mor Ku creek and flow out to Mae Ork Hu creek and Mei river, causing the natural water source to be contaminated by the wastewater. However, if there is enough distance between the water source and wastewater collecting area, the wastewater flowing from the shelter can become naturally filtered (Fig. 4.77).

Fig. 4.78 Garbage founded on the ground shows disorderly garbage dumping. *Source* Photo taken by study team

Fig. 4.79 Water resource contaminated with pile of garbage. *Source* Photo taken by study team

Fig. 4.80 How to destroy garbage: separate garbage ready for recycle; dry garbage burning. *Source* Photo taken by study team

Impacts from the Garbage Disposal System

The survey and the questioning of COERR authorities show denizens put garbage in bags which are kept in the arranged areas, then the garbage is taken by authorities for disposal. Although the denizens keep the garbage in the bags orderly, the garbage can be seen on the ground. That not only causes the scenery to be ugly but also becomes the source for diseases. Random garbage dumping has resulted in a contaminated river because garbage was blown by rain and storms. The water quantity in the creek has also been affected (Figs. 4.78 and 4.79).

The weight of dumped garbage in the garbage pit is around 20,000–23,000 kg/week. Garbage is mostly plastic, glass and paper. Some recycling does take place; around 1,000 kg/month of plastic and glass is recycled by burning in an incinerator, and other dry garbage, 200 kg/day, is also burned. Some garbage remains in the pit; a great amount of garbage scatters on the ground and flows into the river (Fig. 4.80).

4.7 Environmental Impacts Outside the Displaced Persons' Temporary Settlement

4.7.1 Around Ban Tham Hin

4.7.1.1 Water Related Impacts

Ban Tham Hin shelter area is steep and located in the high land. The river that is close to and flows to the shelter is Nam Khun creek, located in the lower area. Used water flows into Huay Nam Khun and has a bad effect on water in the creek. Water from Nam Khun creek will flow into the Ban Thum Hin reservoir and then

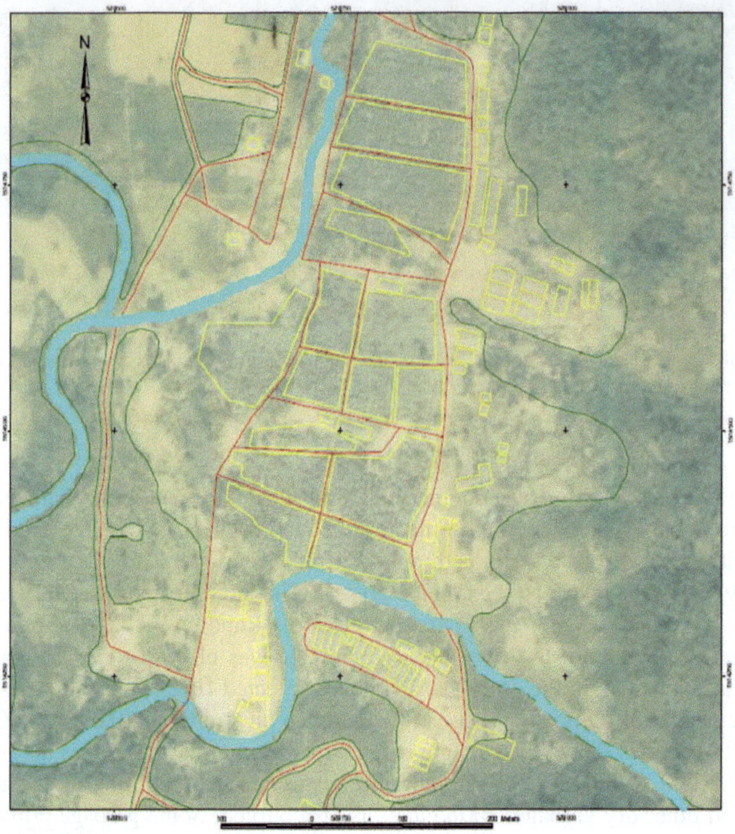

Fig. 4.81 The location of Nam Khun creek near shelter and support wasted water. *Source* The Authors

to Klum creek, the important river of Ban Thum Hin and surrounding area. The water flows through Ban Thum Hin, Ban Som Phoy, Ban Huay Klum before flowing into Phashe which is the important river of plateau. Phashe river will flow to join Saiyok river in Khanjanaburee (Figs. 4.81 and 4.82).

The water environment from the shelter can connect to the outside area because of the water flows. Therefore, flowing of wasted water from consumption and from waste washing affects the surrounding area and the waterway area. Wasted water that comes from denizens was calculated 174,220 l/day from 8,711 of denizens, almost equal to the number of people in Tambon Saunphung which is 10,555 people. Because there are a great number of people living in the limited area, the density is very high. Management of public health and the environment is inadequate. Pollution and a poor environment causes the river to be dirty and leads to the epidemics to the outside area. The effects could be widespread because the waterway is extensive. Moreover, the wasted waterway could run through the

Fig. 4.82 Direction of water flowing from the shelter to the outside area. *Source* The Authors

village in Tumbon Suanphung to Triyok river in Kanjanaburee. Since the waterway is extensive, and there are rivers and creeks flowing into the waterway, dirt from wasted water can be decreased and natural water therapy can be done.

Impacts from Garbage

There are effects from garbage impact in surrounding areas directly outside the shelter. The effects from garbage are terrible scenery, air pollution and bad odour from garbage and garbage burning. In some areas, the garbage zone is close to the river or road, disease and dirt can easily be transferred.

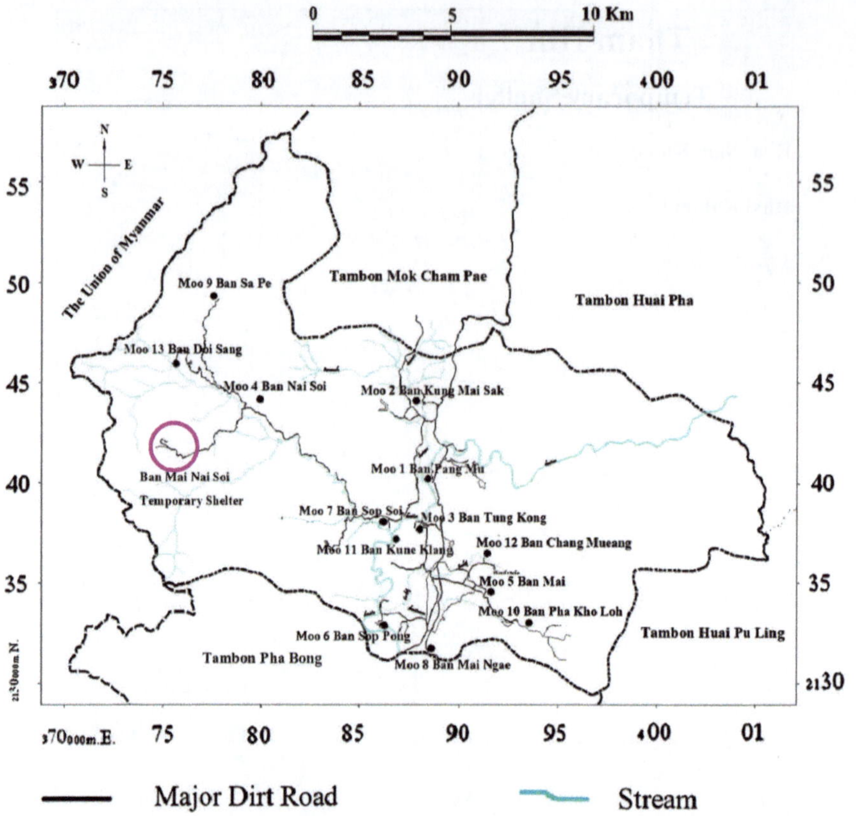

Fig. 4.83 Tumbon Pangmoo map shows the connecting areas of environment and Waterway. *Source* Adapted from the Mae Hong Son urban planning office, Ministry of Interior

4.7.2 Around Ban Mai Nai Soy

Environment effects occur in surrounding areas of the shelter. Displaced persons compete for resources with local people, and activities affect environment quality such as releasing wastewater and garbage dumping. The number of the displaced persons is 15,341 (TBBC 2010), which is the same as the population in Tumbon Pangmu, and eight times of the population in Naisoy village. The areas surrounding shelter in Moo4 Bannaisoy, Moo13 Bandoisang and Moo9 Banmaisapae are the nearest areas to the shelter; these areas get the environment effects more than the far away areas (Fig. 4.83).

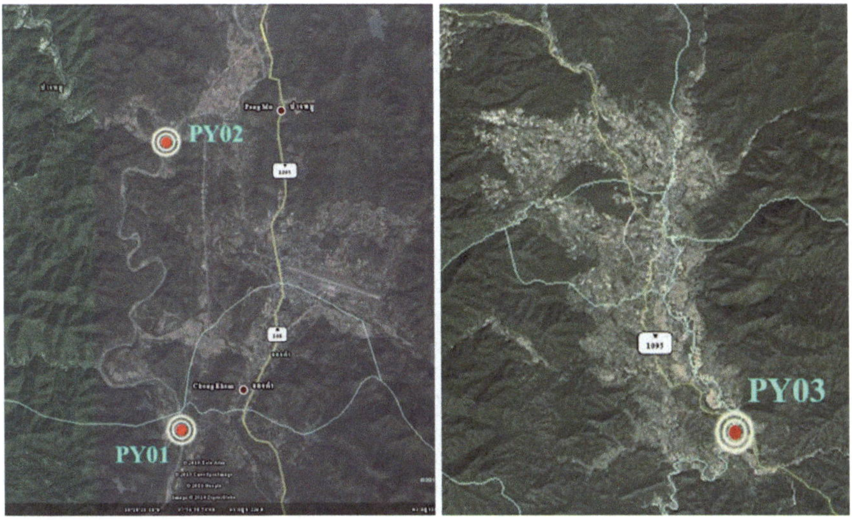

Fig. 4.84 Quality measurement points of Pai River. *Source* The Authors

4.7.2.1 Water-Related Impacts

The shelter is located in the riverhead forest and Pong Creek flows through the shelter and small rivers in the area. This factor causes the wastewater that had flown through the rivers to run into Pong Creek that flows through the shelter to meet Soy River in Ban Nai Soy in the East. Soy River will flow to meet Pai River in Sob Soy village and then flows through Ban Khun Klang, Ban Sop Pong before Pai River flow to meet Salawin River in Myanmar. Wastewater from the displaced persons' activities might contaminate river and flow through the waterway. Villages located at the end of the tide that get the effects from wastewater are Naisoy village, Khunklang village and Sobpong village. Wastewater from the displaced persons is overall 617,240 l/day. This number is considered high because its quantity is equal to waste from the whole population in Tumbon Pang Moo. Wastewater from the shelter comes from the water used by displaced persons in consumption, excreting, breeding animals and cleansing of wasted land surface to the creek.

Mae Hong Son environment office investigated water quality of Pai River in three stations (Fig. 4.84).

Checking in 2009 showed that Pai River had a terrible, quality especially in March to August because of the high contamination of Coliform Bacteria, with water quality in type 4, where such water can be used for industry and consumption if it has been pasteurised and has been through quality development process. Water quality checking in 2010 showed that Department of Educational Agriculture station of Ban Tha Pong is quite good and moderate, namely water quality in type 2 and 3. It is shown that water quality of Department of Educational

Table 4.1 The result from water in Pai River quality analysis in 2009–2010

Station	Month/Year	DO (mg/l)	BOD (mg/l)	TCB (MPN/100 ml)	FCB (MPN/100 ml)	Water quality	Index
PY01	March 2009	8.1	1.1	50,000	17,000	4	TCB, FCB
	May 2009	6.1	2.9	22,000	1,100	4	TCB
	August 2009	6.9	0.6	≥ 160,000	800	4	TCB
	December 2009	8.5	<0.5	9,000	700	3	
	February 2010	8.7	<0.5	1,100	500	2	
	May 2010	6.2	0.9	8,000	400	3	
PY02	August 2009	7.1	1.0	900,000	200	4	TCB
	December 2009	8.6	<0.5	2,400	500	2	
	February 2010	8.7	0.8	5,000	1,100	3	
	May 2010	6.0	4.2	3,000	400	5	BOD
PY03	August 2009	6.5	1.1	≥ 160,000	13,000	4	TCB, FCB
	December 2009	8.3	<0.5	3,000	800	2	
	February 2010	9.3	1.2	14,000	9,000	4	FCB
	May 2010	7.6	1.3	11,000	900	3	

Source Environment office, Mae Hong Son

Agriculture station is better than in 2009 because wastewater was cleansed by rain in the rainy season of 2009. However, water quality becomes worse in the following year because there is a little water in the rivers during the wintertime. However, the quantity of wasted water remains the same. The effectiveness of natural water therapy is worse than when the water is full. The water quality in Prang Moo official division station is between moderate and terrible, as is Chiangmai-Pai bridge road station. Contamination of Faecal Coliform Bacteria is found highly in February (Table 4.1).

The Pai River is contaminated by Coliform Bacteria. These bacteria come from waste excreting of humans and animals, with a large population and a high density in each area leading to poor environment quality if these factors are not well managed. Exact causes of the poor quality of Pai River cannot be assigned, but the shelter located in the riverhead area. Wastewater might affect to the water in waterway before flowing into Pai River. If the population in the shelter becomes larger and the wastewater management is not effective, these can affect water quality.

Impacts from Garbage

For the garbage in Ban Mai Nai Soy shelter which is buried as landfill, concrete is built in the mountain groove in order to fence the garbage from the water. The effect from the garbage that would occur in the surrounding areas in terms of the garbage flowing from the landfill in the shelter to the surrounding areas is hardly happened. However, garbage dumping behaviour of the displaced persons might affect the surrounding area by the rain pouring and wiping garbage on the ground into the creeks. That causes the terrible scenery of water resource and garbage areas; there is a lot of garbage that is left around the landfill areas. Such areas are the breeding grounds for diseases carried by animals, as indicated by the large number of flies that appear around the landfills. If the public health system in the area is not effective, the diseases can be spread rapidly and might spread to the areas outside the shelter.

In addition, the garbage problem connects to water quality. Contamination of garbage in the river can cause poor water quality problem, especially if the garbage is organic and likely to easily decompose.

The effects from environment and garbage problems from the shelter are less clear than in Ban Mae Lha shelter, perhaps due to the difference between physical characteristics of the areas.

4.7.3 Around Ban Mae La

The study shows that problems are mostly from the displaced persons and affect the environment and people who live in the surrounding areas. The main cause of the problems is the number of the displaced persons, which are more than 46,392 people. This amount is larger than in Ban Mae Lha areas, which are 7,566 people. The number of the displaced persons is six times higher, causing considerable waste per day from the displaced persons' activities. In addition, the environment management of the shelter and the crowded area give the displaced persons a poor quality of life. The resource using and garbage dumping behaviour of the displaced persons are linked to their survival rather than concerns for environment problems.

The physical characteristic of Ban Mae Lha area and natural resources there are the waterways that connect the shelter and Ban Mae Lha area, including the communities in Ban Mae Lha that are not far from the shelter. The displaced

Fig. 4.85 Creek is blocked by sandbags to retain water to use in the shelter. *Source* The Authors

Fig. 4.86 The investigated area and the water physical characteristic in Mae Ork Hu creek. *Source* The Authors

persons' activities in the shelter affect surrounding areas. The environment effects in the shelter area can divide into two parts, which are water effects and water quality garbage effects.

4.7.3.1 Water Related Impacts

There are two mains issues of water effects caused by the evacuee' activities, which are water shortages and water quality problem. The displaced persons use water from Mae Ork Hu creek, which is important to people in Moo1, Moo3, Moo4 and Moo9 of Ban Mae Lha. This creek is normally used for consumption and agricultural (Mae Lha Sub district Administration Organisation). The creek is blocked by sandbags to trap water to use in the shelter. Such a method affects water used in the surrounding areas in the end of a tide because water in Hae Ork Hu creek is used, especially if there is a little water during the wintertime (Fig. 4.85).

The physical characteristic of Mae Ork Hu creek is investigated in Moo3, Ban Mae Ork Pha Roo. The waterway flows through the shelter and flows to meet Maey River. A was done on 2 September 2010, during the rainy season. The result finds that PH value in the water is 7.68 equal to 427 μs and the temperature is at 25 °C. The water quality is muddy with brown colour. Water level is high and flow heavily (Fig. 4.86).

There is a connection on the waterway of Mae Ork Hu that flows through the shelter in C zone and is combined with Shi Mor Ku creek. Chi Mor Go is a creek that flows throughout the shelter from A–C zone. Water in Mae Ork Hu creek that is combined with Shi Mor Ku creek would flow to Moo9 Ban Mae Ork Hu and Moo3 Ban Mae Ork Pha Roo before flowing into Maey River in Moo3, Ban Mae Ork Pha Roo. The connection between the shelter and the surrounding areas is

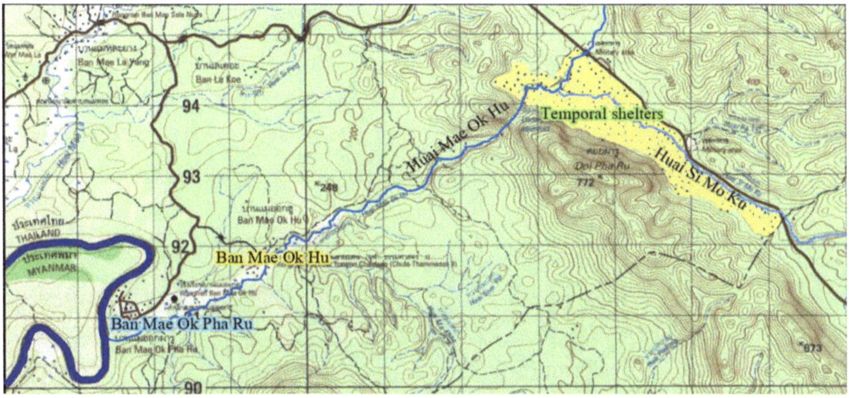

Fig. 4.87 The waterway that connects to the shelter and the surrounding areas. *Source* The Authors

Fig. 4.88 Wastewater characteristic in Mae Ork Hu. *Source* Photo by study team

polluted. The quantity of wasted water from consumption is 1,855,680 l/day. Wastewater quantity from pollution cleansing would flow to Mae Ork Hu creek and affect to water quality in Mae Ork Hu creek including Maey River. Especially, water from Mae Ork Hu becomes green and yellow in the wintertime. That indicates wastewater. Because of the high quantity of water which flows into the water sources with only a little quantity of diluted water, the water quality becomes terrible (interview). The waste cleansing is also found in the wintertime. It is clearly seen that the great quantity of garbage flowing into the creeks causes diseases and affects water quality.

Water pollution has an effect on water using in the areas. People who live at the tail end of a tide that connects to the shelter cannot use the water from Mae Ork Hu for consumption and for agriculture. Moreover, people drink water from sand pit near the creeks without boiling, with consequences for their health. The information from public health found that the diseases that occur in the population in the areas are alimentary canal disease such as diarrhoea (Figs. 4.87 and 4.88).

Fig. 4.89 Garbage in the landfill. *Source* Photo by study team

Fig. 4.90 The route to landfill that is close to the road. *Source* Photo by study team

Fig. 4.91 Black rubber silk is laid at the bottom of a landfill. *Source* Photo by study team

Fig. 4.92 Landfill full of garbage. *Source* Photo by study team

Fig. 4.93 Effect from garbage from the shelter: garbage flowing with the water; garbage flowing into the rice fields in rainy season. *Source* Photo by study team

Impacts from Garbage

Landfill area and the incinerator are in Moo2 Ban Mae Lha Yang. The landfill is around 20 × 50 × 10 m. Landfill is used by the displaced persons and local people in Ban Mae Lha. Because the number of the displaced persons is six times larger than local people, the quantity of garbage in the landfill that comes from the displaced persons is higher than from local people. Garbage from the shelter is around 2,857–3,286 kg/day. After garbage is destroyed by recycling and burnt, the amount of leftover garbage in the landfill is 2,624–3,053 kg/day, less than the quantity of destroyed garbage. There is a considerable quantity of the leftover garbage in the landfill of Moo2 Ban Mae Lha Yang. In addition, the waste garbage leads to diseases and causes offensive smells and unpleasant scenery because the landfill is close to the local road. Epidemics can be spread, especially when it rains. The rain will wipe the garbage spreading throughout the areas and that will affect the health of people who live in the surrounding area.

At Ban Mae Lha shelter, it was found that there is some garbage blown off the road. The wastewater that collects in the landfill is let off in the rainy season causing the wastewater to flow into the creek that people use for consumption. Although black rubber silk is laid at the bottom of a landfill in order to stop pollutants contaminating the soil and water, contamination still occurs because the area outside the landfill is full of garbage. The garbage will be discomposed and become wastewater and will be wiped by rain into natural water sources and surrounding areas causing problems to the environment (Figs. 4.89, 4.90, 4.91 and 4.92).

Apart from the pollution from garbage in the landfill, there is still some garbage dumping into the natural water source in the shelter and wiping garbage into water sources which is Mae Ork Hu creek. That causes water pollution. Garbage will flow with the water in the creek into the end of the tide area. Especially in the rainy season, the garbage will be wiped into the rice field of local people and affect water consumption and agriculture with bacteria found in rice (information from the Sub District Administration Organisation Authorities Mae Lha interview) (Fig. 4.93).

Reference

TBBC, 2010: *Burmese Border Refugee Sites with Population Figures*. http://www.tbbc.org/camps/2010-06-jun-map-tbbc-unhcr.pdf.

Chapter 5
Humanitarian Assistance and Displaced Peoples' Perception of Environmental Issues in the Shelters

Suwattana Thadaniti, Kanokphan U-Sha, Bart Lambregts, Jaturapat Bhiromkaew, Saowanee Wijitkosum, Vollop Prombang and Suchaow Toommakorn

Abstract Humanitarian assistance aims to provide a basic standard of living to the displaced people, with enough food and shelter, and to provide them with a living environment that is safe, clean and adequate, including clean water, washing and bathing facilities. In general, displaced persons rate the support they have had as good, including services provided to them such as waste disposal. However, given the length of time that has elapsed and the number of displaced persons, together with the competition with the local Thai population, assistance is being strained, and issue such as solid waste disposal is reaching crisis point. The shelters are becoming increasingly overcrowded, polluted and noisy, and tensions are rising accordingly, especially amongst young people, who are less compliant and more impatient. Measures are needed at local level to maintain and improve the environment; and the root cause of the arrival of displaced persons needs to be addressed.

S. Thadaniti (✉)
Social Research Institute, Chulalongkorn University, Bangkok, Thailand
e-mail: tsuwattana@yahoo.com

K. U-Sha
Institute of Asian Studies, Chulalongkorn University, Bangkok, Thailand

B. Lambregts
Division of Urban and Environmental Planning, Faculty of Architecture, Kasetsart University, Bangkok, Thailand

J. Bhiromkaew
Royal Thai Police, Bangkok, Thailand

S. Wijitkosum
Environmental Research Institute, Chulalongkorn University, Bangkok, Thailand

V. Prombang
Royal Thai survey department, Bangkok, Thailand

S. Toommakorn
Pisut Technology Consultant Company, Bangkok, Thailand

S. Thadaniti and S. Chantavanich (eds.), *The Impact of Displaced People's Temporary Shelters on Their Surrounding Environment*, SpringerBriefs in Environment, Security, Development and Peace 16, DOI: 10.1007/978-3-319-02842-2_5,

Keywords Refugee survey · Noise pollution · Air pollution · Water pollution · Refugee opinions · Washing facilities · Latrines · Waste disposal · NGOs

5.1 Introduction

So far this report has explored the state of affairs with regard to the environmental quality in and around the temporary shelters and the displaced peoples' way of living and the accompanying use of natural resources. This chapter looks into the sufficiency of the humanitarian assistance and peoples' responses to it, and the displaced peoples' perception of the quality of the environment in which they live. It concludes with a discussion of health issues. Data for this chapter were collected by means of a field survey.

5.2 Humanitarian Assistance and the Environment

UNHCR is the principal organisation providing assistance to displaced persons in Thailand. In addition, there is a wide variety of NGOs and international organisations providing all kinds of specialised services and support inside the shelters and beyond. A number of them together form the Committee for Coordination of Services to Displaced Persons in Thailand (CCSDPT). CCSDPT plays a major role in facilitating discussions, information sharing and providing guidance to relevant Thai agencies. Since 2004, CCSDPT and UNHCR have worked in close coordination, including seeking additional funding from major donors and finding ways to improve the quality of life, well-being and livelihood for the displaced persons with the Royal Thai Government (RTG) (Table 5.1).

5.3 Sufficiency of Supplies and Responses

By leading their daily life, people tend to affect the environment. This is true for the displaced people living in the temporary shelters along the Thai-Burmese border. Conditions for this group of people, however, are special: displaced

Table 5.1 Overview of the NGOs working in the area of environmental protection in the three temporary shelters

Environmental Issues	Ban Mae La	Ban Nai Soi	Ban Thum Hin
Waste management	COERR	IRC	IRC
Sanitation and water management	AMI SOLIDARITIES	IRC	IRC
Food, shelter and non-food items	TBBC	TBBC	TBBC
Environmental protection campaigns	COERR	COERR	COERR

Source The authors

persons generally face severe restrictions in the management of their daily lives and livelihoods and depend on humanitarian assistance for many aspects. From the survey and observations, it was learned that these restrictions provoke responses that actually aggravate environmental impacts. For instance, insufficient supply of sustainable building materials provokes uncontrolled collection of additional materials with possible negative environmental impacts. The supply of cooking fuel types that displaced people are unfamiliar with, such as synthetic charcoal, may unintentionally lead to searches for firewood instead. Prolonged dependence on monotonous dried food rations consisting of rice, *mung* beans, dried chillies and iodised salt also makes people crave for a change.

These and other factors entice some displaced people into exposing themselves to the risk of arrest by leaving the shelters to collect certain resources or find additional food items, which may happen in environmentally unsustainable ways. Besides the problems caused by insufficiency of provided resources and monotonousness, the displaced people's behaviour, notably in dealing with waste, generates environmental impacts too, both inside the shelters and outside, affecting the local community living close by the camps.

5.3.1 Food Supply

Findings from the survey show that respondents from three shelters did not only receive food basket from the TBBC, but they depended heavily upon TBBC's general assistance as well. A large majority of the respondents live off the TBBC's assistance, but the findings disclose that the composition of food basket was designed to give a proper balance of calorie and provided similar items of dried food in order to ensure the basic nutritional needs for living for more than 10 years. As a result, the displaced people had an increasing need for fresh food, especially fresh vegetables and meat. The respondents also mentioned their needs for other food items such as fresh fish and fruit (Tables 5.2 and 5.3).

Wages from work are a major source of income that the respondents from three shelters use to buy fresh food. About 42 % of the respondents in Ban Tham Hin, 30 % of the respondents in Ban Mae La and 27 % of the respondents in Ban Mai Nai Soi used their wages to buy fresh food. The secondary source of fresh food was from looking outside the temporary shelters, growing food inside the temporary shelter and raising livestock inside the temporary shelter. Some respondents used

Table 5.2 Does your household receive the food basket provided by TBBC

Does your household receive the food basket provided by TBBC?	Tham Hin		Ban Mai Nai Soi		Ban Mae la	
	Number	Percent	Number	Percent	Number	Percent
(1) No	3	2.8	2	2.0	22	9.9
(2) Yes	105	97.2	100	98.0	201	90.1
Total	108	100	102	100	223	100

Source The authors

Table 5.3 What additional food item not included in the TBBC food basket does your household need most?

What additional food item not included in the TBBC food basket does your household need most?	Ban Mae la		Ban Mai Nai Soi		Tham Hin	
	Number	Percent	Number	Percent	Number	Percent
(1) Fresh vegetables	82	37.1	28	27.7	21	18.9
(2) Fruit	30	13.6	11	10.9	8	7.2
(3) Red Meat	52	23.5	38	37.6	51	46.0
(4) Fish	45	20.4	15	14.9	14	12.6
(5) Other	12	5.4	9	8.9	13	11.7
Total	221	100	101	100	107	100

Table 5.4 Has your family ever gotten food in the following ways?

Has your family ever gotten food in the following ways?	Ban Mae la		Ban Mai Nai Soi		Tham Hin	
	Number	Percent	Number	Percent	Number	Percent
(1) Growing food inside the temporary shelter	76	13.5	41	12.8	29	13.9
(2) Raising livestock inside the temporary shelter	77	13.7	71	22.2	4	1.9
(3) Looking for food outside the temporary shelter	88	15.6	63	19.7	33	15.9
(4) Bartering/trading goods	46	8.2	25	7.8	12	5.8
(5) Buying food with income	167	29.7	87	27.2	87	41.8
(6) Buying food with money sent from friends or relatives outside the temporary shelter	53	9.4	20	6.3	25	12.0
(7) Food provided by community-based organisations	34	6.0	11	3.4	15	7.2
(8) Other	22	3.9	2	0.6	3	1.4
Total	563[a]	100	320[a]	100	208[a]	100

Source The authors
[a] Respondents were allowed to give more than one answer

money received from friends or relatives living outside the temporary shelter to buy fresh food (Table 5.4).

On the top of the food basket supplied by TBBC, the displaced people of all three shelters also maintained *kitchen gardens* for family consumption. This kind of small-scale gardening not only helps displaced people to get some fresh and more varied food, but is also a way of supplementing TBBC rations to have enough food for all members of family. Gardening is typically done around the house, in the forest area near the shelters and in agricultural areas allotted by the private organisation (Tables 5.5 and 5.6).

For livestock, it is found that 94 % of the respondents in Ban Tham Hin and 59 % of the respondents in Ban Mae La did not raise any livestock. Meanwhile 84 % of the respondents in Ban Mai Nai Soi and 41 % of the respondents in Ban

Table 5.5 Have you and your family done any gardening?

You and your family have done any gardening?	Ban Mae la		Ban Mai Nai Soi		Tham Hin	
	Number	Percent	Number	Percent	Number	Percent
(1) No	140	62.8	54	53.5	89	78.8
(2) Yes	83	37.2	47	46.5	24	21.2
The place done any gardening						
– close to my house	77	92.8	37	78.7	3	12.5
– in the forest	–	–	5	10.6	4	16.7
– in the arranged vacant space	4	4.8	2	4.3	12	50.0
– other	2	2.4	3	6.4	5	20.8
Total	223	100	101	100	113	100

Source The authors

Table 5.6 Have you ever been trained to do farming or gardening?

Have you ever been trained to farming or gardening?	Ban Mae la		Ban Mai Nai Soi		Tham Hin	
	Number	Percent	Number	Percent	Number	Percent
(1) No	149	66.8	63	64.3	80	70.8
(2) Yes	74	33.2	35	35.7	33	29.2
Total	223	100	98	100	113	100

Source The authors

Table 5.7 Did you raise any livestock?

Did you raise any livestock?	Ban Mae la		Ban Mai Nai Soi		Tham Hin	
	Number	Percent	Number	Percent	Number	Percent
(1) No	132	59.2	16	15.8	105	93.8
(2) Yes	91	40.8	85	84.2	7	6.3
The place raise livestock						
– close to my house	87	95.6	84	98.8	–	–
– in the forest	–	–	1	1.2	–	–
– in the arranged vacant space	2	2.2	–	–	7	100
– other	2	2.2	–	–	–	–
Total	223	100	101	100	112	100

Source The authors

Mae La raised their own livestock. The livestock raised was chicken, pig, goat and cow (Table 5.7).

5.3.2 Housing

It was found that 90 % of the respondents in Ban Mai Nai Soi and 80 % of the respondents in Ban Tham Hin built their own houses. Some respondents,

Table 5.8 Did you or your family members build your own house?

Building your own house	Ban Mae la		Ban Mai Nai Soi		Tham Hin	
	Number	Percent	Number	Percent	Number	Percent
(1) No	65	29.2	8	7.9	13	11.5
(2) Yes	158	70.9	93	92.1	100	88.5
Total	223	100	101	100	113	100

Source The authors

particularly in Ban Mae La, did not build their own houses. About 29 % of the respondents moved into their relatives' or other families' houses, as the home-owners resettled to a third country (Table 5.8).

TBBC provided construction materials to the displaced people. Noticeably, 32 % of the respondents in Ban Mai Nai Soi together with 13 % of the respondents in Ban Mae La got their building materials from the local forests. Apart from this, some respondents received their building materials from donors (Table 5.9).

As to the sufficiency of building materials supplied by the TBBC, the findings showed that 68 % of the respondents in Ban Mae La and 54 % of the respondents in Ban Tham Hin received enough building materials. Meanwhile 64 % of the respondents in Ban Mai Nai Soi had inadequate material supplied (Table 5.10).

Besides all the essential construction materials supplied, the respondents still needed other building materials as well. In Ban Mae La, bamboo, wood and thatch were most needed by the respondents. In Ban Mai Nai Soi, thatch, bamboo and Eucalyptus poles were most needed. In Ban Tham Hin, thatch, bamboo and Eucalyptus poles were most needed (Table 5.11).

Table 5.9 Apart from TBBC, where else did you get the construction materials?

From where did you get the construction material?	Ban Mae la		Ban Mai Nai Soi		Tham Hin	
	Number	Percent	Number	Percent	Number	Percent
(1) From donors	9	5.7	5	5.4	18	19.0
(2) Cut from the forest	21	13.3	30	32.3	6	6.3
(3) Both (1) and (2)	3	1.9	1	1.1	4	4.2
(4) From only TBBC	77	48.7	33	35.5	67	70.5
(5) Other	48	30.4	24	25.8	–	–
Total	158	100	93	100	95	100

Source The authors

Table 5.10 Did you receive enough shelter items provided by TBBC?

Did you receive enough shelter items provided by TBBC?	Ban Mae La		Ban Mai Nai Soi		Tham Hin	
	Number	Percent	Number	Percent	Number	Percent
(1) Yes	147	67.7	36	35.6	55	53.9
(2) No	70	32.3	65	64.4	47	46.1
Total	217	100	101	100	102	100

Source The authors

Table 5.11 Which shelter items does your household need most?

Which shelter items does your household need most?	Ban Mae La		Ban Mai Nai Soi		Tham Hin	
	Number	Percent	Number	Percent	Number	Percent
(1) Bamboo	85	38.1	27	26.7	27	26.5
(2) Thatch	37	16.6	33	32.7	33	32.4
(3) Eucalyptus poles	25	11.2	21	20.8	21	20.6
(4) Nails	3	1.4	3	3.0	3	2.9
(5) Plastic roofing	18	8.1	4	4.0	4	4.0
(6) Wood	51	22.9	10	9.9	10	9.8
(7) Mud	2	0.9	–	–	3	3.0
(8) Other	2	0.9	3	3.0	1	1.0
Total	223	100	101	100	102	100

Source The authors

5.3.3 Cooking Fuel

Cooking fuel in the form of synthetic charcoal is supplied by the TBBC. The findings indicate that only a few respondents used the charcoal provided. Most of them were familiar with other cooking fuels such as wood, bamboo and other cooking fuels, and continued to use these (Table 5.12).

5.3.4 Garbage Disposal

For garbage disposal by the displaced people in their daily life, 90 % of the respondents in Ban Mae La and 74 % of the respondents in Ban Mai Nai Soi and 65 % of Ban Tham Hin abided by the rule of NGO garbage management. Most disposed of their garbage and waste at the disposal areas provided. However, the findings also point out that some respondents, especially those living in Ban Mai Nai Soi and Ban Tham Hin, threw their garbage away at the nearby yard around their houses (Table 5.13).

Table 5.12 Apart from the charcoal, what else do you use for cooking?

What else do you use for cooking?	Ban Mae la		Ban Mai Nai Soi		Tham Hin	
	Number	Percent	Number	Percent	Number	Percent
(1) Charcoal	41	18.4	7	6.8	43	38.1
(2) Wood (specify from where)	93	41.7	88	86.3	48	42.5
(3) Other, specify	89	39.9	7	6.9	22	19.5
Total	223	100	102	100	113	100

Source The authors

Table 5.13 How do you dispose your garbage?

How do you dispose your garbage?	Ban Mae la		Ban Mai Nai Soi		Tham Hin	
	Number	Percent	Number	Percent	Number	Percent
(1) By NGO management	201	90.1	74	74.0	74	65.5
(2) Throw away at the nearby yard	16	7.2	25	25.0	26	23.0
(3) Recycle/reused (specify how)	1	0.5	1	1.0	13	11.5
(4) Other	5	2.2	–	–	–	–
Total	223	100	100	100	113	100

Source The authors

5.4 Displaced People's Perception of the Environmental Quality in the Shelters

5.4.1 Physical Environment

People were asked to value the physical conditions in their shelter and compare the situation with their previous living environment in Myanmar. In Ban Mai Nai Soi, 52 % of the respondents considered the physical conditions comfortable. In Ban Mae La, 46 % of the respondents thought the current physical conditions better than the conditions they faced in Myanmar. In Ban Tham Hin, 35 % of the respondents considered the physical conditions as being not too bad. As for the natural environment, both Ban Mae La and Ban Mai Nai Soi are considered by the displaced people to have a fertile natural environment. However, in Ban Tham Hin, respondents considered the natural environment surrounding the shelter very dry (Tables 5.14 and 5.15).

Table 5.14 What is the physical condition in your camp?

Physical condition	Ban Mae la		Ban Mai Nai Soi		Tham Hin	
	Number	Percent	Number	Percent	Number	Percent
(1) Very comfortable	37	16.6	9	8.9	5	4.4
(2) Comfortable	51	22.9	53	52.5	36	31.9
(3) Not too bad	33	14.8	6	5.9	39	34.5
(4) Better than my home in Myanmar	102	45.7	33	32.7	32	28.3
(5) No opinion	–	–	–	–	1	0.9
Total	223	100	101	100	113	100

Source The authors

Table 5.15 How is the natural environment surrounding your camp location?

How is the natural environment surrounding your camp?	Ban Mae la		Ban Mai Nai Soi		Tham Hin	
	Number	Percent	Number	Percent	Number	Percent
(1) Very fertile	21	9.4	8	7.9	2	1.8
(2) Fertile	149	66.8	56	55.5	16	14.3
(3) Dry	45	20.2	35	34.7	43	38.4
(4) Very dry	8	3.6	2	2.0	51	45.5
Total	223	100	101	100	112	100

Source The authors

5.4.2 Perceived Pollution Inside the Shelter and Its Sources

Smell pollution is reported to be the worst kind of pollution in all three temporary shelters, followed by noise pollution and air pollution (Table 5.16).

5.4.2.1 Source of Pollution: Smell

In Ban Mai Nai Soi, smell pollution in the shelter came from waste paper, plastic, animal remains and animal droppings such as chicken and pig, garbage, wastewater around the house, water retained in the area of water distribution station, toilets inside the houses together with the next door's toilet and cooking.

In Ban Mae La, smell pollution in the shelter was from garbage breeze, garbage burning, animal droppings such as pig, chicken, goat and cow raised by the residents, wastewater, garbage disposal inside the shelters and toilets. Bad smells also came from smoke emitting from plastic and garbage burning, wildfire, motorcycle, muffler and cooking. Bad smells also emitted from wastewater from a landfill located near the river in B Zone. After the rainy season, the garbage emitted a bad odour, especially when the water has ebbed away.

In Ban Tham Hin, smell pollution in the shelter was from garbage around the shelter, burning, polluted water from the unclean and overcrowded household and cooking. Bad smells also emitted from the polyethylene roofs. This kind of roof tends to produce a bad smell when it warms up under sunshine. Latrines, especially

Table 5.16 What kinds of pollution do you experience in your camps?

What kinds of pollution in your camps?	Ban Mae la		Ban Mai Nai Soi		Tham Hin	
	Number	Percent	Number	Percent	Number	Percent
(1) Noise	37	22.4	24	20.0	31	42.5
(2) Air	20	12.1	25	20.8	–	–
(3) Smell	108	65.5	60	50.0	40	54.8
(4) Other	–	–	11	9.2	2	2.7
Total	165	100	120	100	73	100

Source The Authors

during rainy season when wastewater from the toilet and lavatory overflows the natural cesspits, emitted a very bad smell too.

5.4.2.2 Source of Pollution: Noise

In Ban Mai Nai Soi, most of the noise pollution originated from drunk people talking in loud voices and fighting, motorcycles, noisy conversations between groups of teenagers and children, loud music and from the electric generator. In Ban Mae La, noise in the shelter came from the drunk people talking in loud voices and fighting, noisy conversation between teenagers, musical instruments (guitar), the voices of children in the playground, loud voices from amplifiers used in religious ceremonies, motorcycles and cars. In Ban Tham Hin, noise in the shelter was from drunk people talking in loud voices and fighting, CD players, televisions, electric generators, motorcycles and from children at the playground.

5.4.2.3 Source of Pollution: Air

In Ban Mai Nai Soi, air pollution in the shelter mostly came from the burning of garbage, wood and plastic. Smoke from cooking and wildfires was also a source of air pollution, as was dust, the latter especially for those living next to the road. In Ban Mae La, smoke from garbage burning, wildfire, muffler, motorcycle, burning and dust was reported as a source of air pollution in the shelter. In Ban Tham Hin, smoke from burning, wildfire, garbage burning and dust was the source of air pollution in the shelter.

5.4.3 Perceived Pollution Around the Residential Area and Its Sources

As for perceived pollution around the residential area, smell pollution is reported to be the worst pollution in all three temporary shelters. The secondary pollutions are noise pollution and air pollution (Table 5.17).

Table 5.17 What kinds of pollutions do you perceive around your house?

What kinds of pollutions do you perceive around your house?	Ban Mae la		Ban Mai Nai Soi		Tham Hin	
	Number	Percent	Number	Percent	Number	Percent
(1) Noise	38	23.8	30	24.4	46	40.7
(2) Air	17	10.6	12	9.8	14	12.4
(3) Smell	104	65.0	68	55.3	55	48.7
(4) Other	1	0.6	13	10.6	1	0.90
Total	160	100	123	100		

Source Author survey

5.4.3.1 Source of Pollution: Smell

In Ban Mai Nai Soi, smell pollution around the house was from garbage burning close to the house, animal remains, bad odour from dirty neighbourhood and polluted water from the neighbours. In Ban Mae La, the source of smell pollution around the house was from animal droppings such as chicken, pig and goat; retained sewage; used water flowing from houses located on the top area and wastewater from toilet inside the house and their neighbours. Polluted water in a canal was a source of bad smell, as the garbage was contaminated with water in the rainy season. Thus, when water decreased, garbage emitted bad odour. In Ban Tham Hin, smell pollution around the house was from cooking and toilet (some houses had a dirty toilet). Thus, bad smells emitted around the house, as each house located next to each other. Therefore, there was no fresh air circulation. Bad smell was also from garbage burning beside the house and polluted water stored in the area of the water distribution point.

5.4.3.2 Source of the Pollution: Noise

In Ban Mai Nai Soi, noise pollution around the house was from the drunk who talked with loud voice, electric generators, motorcycles, noisy conversations of teenagers and music.

In Ban Mae La, noise pollution around the house was from the drunk talking with loud voice, electric generators, motorcycles, noisy conversations of teenagers, music and loud voices from amplifiers used for religious ceremonies (Information obtained from 38 respondents). In Ban Tham Hin, noise pollution around the house was from the drunk and fighting, CD players, televisions, electric generators, motorcycles and toys.

5.4.3.3 Source of Pollution: Air

In Ban Mai Nai Soi, air pollution around the house was from garbage burning, animal dropping such as chicken, pig, toilet, dust and wildfire in dry season. In Ban Mae La, air pollution around the house was from garbage burning, animal dropping such as chicken and pig, toilet, dust and smoke. In Ban Tham Hin, air pollution around the house was from cooking, garbage burning and dust.

5.5 Health Impacts

The overcrowded dwellings lead to both environmental and health impacts. The three shelters researched are characterised by overcrowding at both shelter and individual household level. This is reflected in the peoples' perception of

Table 5.18 How do you feel about the size of the space in your camp?

How do feel about the size of the space in your camp?	Ban Mae la		Ban Mai Nai Soi		Tham Hin	
	Number	Percent	Number	Percent	Number	Percent
(1) Very crowded	94	42.2	33	32.7	59	52.2
(2) Crowded	57	25.7	36	35.6	37	32.7
(3) Enough room for every one	72	32.4	32	31.7	14	12.4
(4) Other (specify)	–	–	–	–	3	2.7
Total	223	100	101	100	113	100

Source Author survey

Table 5.19 Have you ever gotten any serious disease/sickness?

Did you ever have gotten any serious disease/sickness?	Ban Mae la		Ban Mai Nai Soi		Tham Hin	
	Number	Percent	Number	Percent	Number	Percent
(1)No	167	74.9	69	69.0	75	66.4
(2) Yes, please identify your disease	56	25.2	31	31.0	38	33.6
Total	223	100	100	100	113	100

Source Author survey

Table 5.20 How do you cure your or your family's sickness?

How do you cure your family sickness?	Ban Mae la		Ban Mai Nai Soi		Tham Hin	
	Number	Percent	Number	Percent	Number	Percent
Use the traditional medicine	12	5.4	1	1.0	4	3.6
Go to see a camp clinic	206	92.4	99	99.0	109	97.3
Get the community help service	1	0.4	–	–	1	0.9
Go to see a doctor in town	4	1.8	–	–	4	3.6
Total	223	100	100	100	118	100

Source Author survey

crowdedness: in each of the three shelters, a large majority considered the shelter to be crowded or very crowded.

Causal relations between the environmental conditions prevailing in the shelters and the health conditions of the inhabitants were not explicitly researched, but it is rather likely that such relations exist. The survey found that more than 30 % of the respondents from all three shelters get sick. In Ban Mai Nai Soi, 55 % of the respondents get sick from dengue fever and malaria. Other diseases were stomachache, brain tumour, mental disorder and injuries from fighting. In Ban Mae La, 58 % of the respondents used to get sick of dengue fever and malaria. The other diseases were high blood pressure, leukaemia, epilepsy, gastric ulcer, mental disorder and asthma. In Ban Tham Hin, 51 % of the respondents used to get sick of dengue fever and malaria. The other diseases were diarrhoea and high blood pressure. For treatment, more than 95 % of the respondents from three shelters would get some treatment from the healthcare provider at each shelter's clinic (Tables 5.18, 5.19 and 5.20).

Chapter 6
Conclusions and Recommendations

Suwattana Thadaniti, Kanokphan U-Sha, Bart Lambregts, Jaturapat Bhiromkaew, Saowanee Wijitkosum, Vollop Prombang and Suchaow Toommakorn

Abstract The shelters are sited in remote, sparsely populated areas, partly because of the proximity to Myanmar. They lack infrastructure, such as robust solid waste disposal systems. Though agencies and the RTG have attempted to manage the settlements and their environments, this is proving increasingly challenging. Recommendations are made to each group of key actors, notably the RTG, humanitarian agencies, local population and the displaced persons themselves. In particular, encouraging greater environmental self-sufficiency amongst the displaced persons, and getting them involved in the planning and use of services, is seen as vital. Integrating the settlement's systems, such as electricity, with national Thai sources, will also help.

Keywords Waste disposal · Solid waste · Liquid waste · Recommendations · Environmental impacts

S. Thadaniti (✉)
Social Research Institute, Chulalongkorn University, Bangkok, Thailand
e-mail: tsuwattana@yahoo.com

K. U-Sha
Institute of Asian Studies, Chulalongkorn University, Bangkok, Thailand

B. Lambregts
Division of Urban and Environmental Planning, Faculty of Architecture, Kasetsart University, Bangkok, Thailand

J. Bhiromkaew
Royal Thai Police, Bangkok, Thailand

S. Wijitkosum
Environmental Research Institute, Chulalongkorn University, Bangkok, Thailand

V. Prombang
Royal Thai survey department, Bangkok, Thailand

S. Toommakorn
Pisut Technology Consultant Company, Bangkok, Thailand

S. Thadaniti and S. Chantavanich (eds.), *The Impact of Displaced People's Temporary Shelters on Their Surrounding Environment*, SpringerBriefs in Environment, Security, Development and Peace 16, DOI: 10.1007/978-3-319-02842-2_6,

6.1 Introduction

This study has produced an overview of environmental issues and impacts associated with displaced peoples' temporary settlements along the Thai–Myanmar border. Out of nine such temporary shelters, three were selected for detailed study: Ban Tham Hin in Ratchaburi province, Ban Mai Nai Soi in Mae Hong Son province and Ban Mae La in Tak province. In each of these shelters, a variety of research methods were used to assess the environmental conditions, analyse displaced peoples' way of living and use of resources and disclose displaced peoples' perceptions of the environmental conditions they face. This concluding chapter summarises the main findings, links impacts with causes and consequences and presents a set of recommendations aimed at tackling the most urgent of problems.

6.2 Main Environmental Impacts, Their Causes and Their Consequences

The three temporary shelters examined are situated in sparsely populated, mountainous, terrain, inside or nearby forest reserves. The mountains and forests produce a variety of natural resources including wood and other vegetable materials, edibles and intricate networks of small rivers and creeks. The areas in which the shelters are located are sparsely populated, but not unpopulated: smaller and larger settlements and villages can be found, home to a mix of Thai and other ethnic groups. Establishing temporary shelters for thousands or even tens of thousands displaced people in such areas is likely to cause environmental impacts, a hypothesis that is corroborated by the findings of the current research.

6.2.1 Use of Natural Resources

The study found that the inhabitants of the temporary shelters tend to collect a variety of resources that are found in the shelters' direct surroundings. These include materials used for the construction and maintenance of dwellings such as bamboo, hardwoods, leaves, edibles used to supplement the food rations supplied by the TBBC or as a livelihood strategy, materials used for cooking and water. Such resources are not always collected in sustainable ways and are collected, moreover, usually in competition with the host communities.

Several reasons could be identified that help to explain displaced people leaving the shelters to collect things from the surrounding areas. The need to collect additional construction materials is created by the RTG policy to only allow the use of non-durable materials in house construction, which creates the need for frequent replacement of construction materials, and by insufficient supply of such materials by the TBBC. In a similar vein, monotonous food rations strong on dry food items create a desire for fresh edibles, some of which can be grown inside the shelter, but with others that are to be found outside. In addition, a mismatch seems to exist between the types of cooking fuel that are supplied by the TBBC and the types that the displaced people prefer to use, resulting again in forages through the surroundings to find alternative cooking fuels. And, finally, the fact that the shelters are not connected to regular water supply systems means all water used must be collected from natural sources in and around the shelters.

In terms of consequences, depletion of resources and the fostering of negative feelings between the host communities and the shelter populations are the most noteworthy. Bamboo, hardwoods and edibles produced by the forest are reportedly not always collected in sustainable ways. In specific cases, this leads to depletion of resources, which in turn may lead to secondary effects such as soil degradation and localised loss of biodiversity. Moreover, depletion of resources creates new problems for the displaced people as the need for such materials is likely to remain current. Where host communities have a need for the same kind of materials, collection and possibly depletion of such materials by displaced people are likely to lead to ill feeling between the two, and reduce the host communities' support for sustaining the temporary shelters in their areas. Real conflicts over scarce resources, such as water in the dry season, have not been reported yet, but may arise in the future. It should be noted though, that it was not possible within the scope of this study to establish for a fact to what extent displaced people can be held accountable and to what degree the local population is responsible for resource depletion in the areas surrounding the shelters.

6.2.2 Emission of Solid and Liquid Wastes

Displaced people produce waste like any population. However, the displaced people in the three temporary shelters studied adequate sanitary infrastructure and waste disposal services. Hence, waste is a problem, not only felt within the shelters, but also outside, especially in villages and settlements located downstream along the creeks and rivers running through the shelters. The problem concerns both solid waste, mostly normal household refuse, and liquid waste. The latter includes both wastewater from kitchen use and wastewater from bathroom use.

Parts of the shelters studied lack adequate sanitation and drainage infrastructure. Latrines sometimes lacked septic tanks and wastewater from kitchen use are often allowed to just run into the streets and off the slopes into the creeks at the shelters' base. Treatment of wastewater is insufficient or non-existing. As a result, natural water sources, both creeks and groundwater, tend to get contaminated, the effects of which are also felt by the people living in villages downstream, who also depend on these water sources.

Within the shelters, important side effects of poor sanitation and drainage infrastructure also include bad smell and health hazards. The RTG's policy to disallow the construction of durable sanitation and drainage infrastructure seems to be an important explanatory factor for this situation.

As for solid waste, NGOs have put considerable effort in organising waste collection and disposal systems. These work to a considerable extent, but field observations also revealed that the waste situation is far from ideal yet. Part of the waste is still randomly dumped inside and near the shelters, and also the official sometimes lack proper measures to prevent contamination of ground and surface water. Some sites were not lined with plastic, with the exception of Ban Mae La, while others were found to be located dangerously close to natural water sources. Unnecessary contamination of ground and surface water is the result, the effects of which are also felt by villagers and farmers living and working downstream. Furthermore, rotting garbage spread across the shelters causes bad smells and attracts vermin and other disease-carrying vectors. The practice of open space trash burning adds to the smell nuisance and moreover entails the danger of producing unhealthy smoke when plastics, Styrofoam packaging materials and other hazardous materials are burned.

The cause for the solid waste problem not only stems from inadequate infrastructure and services: displaced peoples' behaviour is also a factor. As mentioned, all shelters studied have a waste collection and disposal system, but random dumping of waste by the inhabitants still occurs. Interventions aimed at addressing the waste problem should therefore focus on both infrastructure and services improvement *and* behavioural change.

Taken together, the liquid and solid waste burden in and around the shelters is high and seriously negatively affects both the quality of the environment and quality of life inside and outside the shelters, and the health situation for both the displaced people and the host communities living in the downstream areas. An urgent response is needed no luxury.

6.3 Recommendations for Improved Management of Environmental Impacts

By carefully choosing the shelter location, wisely designing the shelter layout, thoughtfully investing in basic infrastructure, smartly setting up management and services systems and, finally, patiently educating the people, the environmental impacts of temporary shelters for displaced people could, in theory, be kept down to a minimum. Unfortunately, conditions in practice rarely if ever are such as to allow for careful planning, generous investing and effective management and education. This also holds true for the temporary shelters located along the Thai–Myanmar border. Whereas many of the environmental problems outlined above probably could have been prevented or at least reduced in magnitude if, for example, the shelters had been located in less isolated and vulnerable areas, or if the layout of the shelters had been better adapted to the topography of the areas, reality prescribes that location and layout are established facts and that problems that may in fact originate from these, must be addressed by means of improvements in the domains of infrastructure, management and services, education and awareness raising.

Our recommendations aim to address both the main environmental issues discussed in this report. Key principles underlying the recommendations are flexibility and self-reliance. As the conditions in the various shelters display important similarities as well as significant differences, flexibility is required in the formulation of the recommendations here to allow for meaningful elaboration and specification at the shelter level in a later stage. Flexibility is also called for to take into account the fact that environmental interests are only one of several defining the living conditions in and around the shelters. Decision-makers will have to consider the weight of each of them and strike a balance. The good thing in this respect is that interventions aimed at improving environmental conditions or reducing environmental impacts, often also can be made to work in favour of social and socio-economic interests. It makes sense to build in flexibility in our recommendations since the temporary shelters, in spite of their protracted status, constitute dynamic entities in dynamic environments. Next year's situation may look very different from today's in many respects, even if no official policy efforts are made to initiate change. Flexibility should help those involved in setting out policies and in managing things on the ground, to master such dynamics.

The promotion of self-reliance among the displaced people, in turn, would seem a laudable goal to adhere to for at least three different reasons. First, those providing humanitarian assistance have at their disposal limited resources and their ability and willingness to continue to provide assistance at similar levels in the years to come cannot be taken for granted. Second, it could help to moderate a situation characterised by dependency and boredom, a situation few people stand to gain from. Third, by making the shelters into more self-reliant places, the burden that currently rests on the shoulders of the RTG could somewhat be reduced, freeing resources for other issues of concern.

6.3.1 Addressing the Use of Natural Resources

1. Reduce displaced peoples' need to collect additional construction materials by allowing the use of durable construction materials and/or by providing more generous supplies of temporary construction materials
2. Reduce displaced peoples' need to collect additional edibles by diversifying food rations or, better even, by giving them more opportunities to grow food by themselves. Increase self-reliance in food production and so reduce the need to venture out in the forests. Educate people about high density food production and sustainable agricultural practices. Consider the provision of additional land, but do not sacrifice primary forest area

3. Reduce displaced peoples' practice to collect additional fuels for cooking by encouraging them more strongly to use the cooking fuels that are actually supplied.

6.3.2 Addressing Waste Issues

4. Address problems associated with liquid waste. Exact strategies and measures should be determined at the shelter level as they depend on topography, shelter layout and available infrastructure
5. Address the problems associated with solid waste with infrastructural measures, selection of new landfill, and management measures and/or measures aimed at provoking behavioural change, for example by means of education and/or systems of punishment and reward. Detailed evaluations of the situation in each of the shelters should be made to determine which combination of measures is most appropriate for each case
6. Connect the shelters to the regular power grid; this would strongly reduce the need for battery use and kerosene, and make noisy generators redundant.

6.3.3 Creating Awareness and Providing Skills

7. Educate and train the shelter inhabitants to solve their environmental problems and issues. This could involve general educational activities aimed at changing environmental-unfriendly behaviour, and more specific, vocational training programmes aimed at providing people with particular skills, for example in construction and agriculture
8. Create awareness among those in command of the displaced people situation that sustainable or environmentally friendly solutions do not necessarily equal 'permanent' solutions and that the benefits of such solutions will not only be felt within the shelters, but also beyond, and not only now, but also in the future
9. Create awareness among those in command that increasing the self-reliance the shelter populations is a way to reduce the burden resting on the shoulders of the RTG and associated powers.

6.3.4 Additional Recommendations

A number of additional recommendations to protect the natural environment and reduce the impacts of the shelters on the nearby communities have furthermore been suggested during this study.

10. Adopt a cooperative policy among related government agencies, NGOs, UNHCR, donors and the displaced themselves to generate an awareness of the

protracted refugee problems and the need to create flexibilities within their policy framework
11. Manage woodland and natural resources in the shelters' area as well as its surrounding area
12. Prepare a roster of displaced people who are specialised in woodwork in each Pok. The roster will be prepared by both Camp Committee and Section Leader and forwarding it to the district unit for further process
13. Invite UNHCR and the related private organisations to confer on any career path activities for the displaced people to earn extra money in a way that they can be overseen and managed
14. Make a map on woodland and natural resources, with an accompanying plan for patrolling to prevent deforestation, especially in the restricted-wood area
15. Explore and define a plan for cultivating young plant and reforestation by allowing the community to get involved in restoring natural resources and its environment
16. Educate the displaced people on law enforcement and its related penalty on deforestation
17. Spread knowledge on environment through the curriculum at all levels of education
18. Support the Internal Income Generation Programme in all the shelters as part of encouraging self-sufficiency
19. Set up an Agricultural Programme as a source of food and income, renting the shelter's entrance area for 20–30 rais from the Thai landlord
20. Set up a Reforestation Program by hiring displaced people to plant and take care of the trees
21. Set up a Green Charcoal Factory Programme, bringing the know-how from TBBC projects on the Community Agricultural Nutrition (CAN) to put into practice.

The authors can provide more details on these recommendations and their implementation.

Appendix A: Sampling and Displaced People's Profile

This appendix sketches the profile of the displaced people occupying centre stage in this study. It presents a wide array of basic characteristics and explains how sampling took place.

Sampling for the Baseline Survey

The six studies on livelihood, social welfare and security, environmental impacts, asylum policy, roles of donors, the UN, NGOs and IGOs and resettlement formed two teams during data collection. Team A comprised the livelihood, the social welfare and the environmental impact studies, and team B comprised the other three studies. Splitting-up into two teams was helpful in managing and operating the questionnaire as it reduced its length and the time required for completion. To complete one questionnaire interview took approximately 30–40 min.

In order to define the samplings size, each team applied Yamane's (1967) formula as follows:

$$n = \frac{N}{1 + e^2 N}$$

where

N Element of population, in this study was 145,786.
e Error of sampling, in this study was 5 % or 0.05 proportion.
n Sample size.

Substitution of this formula produces the following result:

$$n = \frac{145,786}{1 + 145,786(0.05)^2} = 400 \text{ displaced persons for each team.}$$

S. Thadaniti and S. Chantavanich (eds.), *The Impact of Displaced People's Temporary Shelters on Their Surrounding Environment*, SpringerBriefs in Environment, Security, Development and Peace 16, DOI: 10.1007/978-3-319-02842-2,

Table A.1 Sample size by location and research team

Temporary shelters	Team A	Team B	Total
Tham Hin	100	100	200
Ban Mai Nai Soi	100	100	200
Mae La	200	200	400
Total	400	400	800

Source Survey data

Therefore, the two teams collected information from 800 displaced persons who were randomly selected from the three temporary settlements. Table A.1 gives the breakdown per settlement. The sample accounts for variety in terms of gender, ethnicity, legal status within the shelter (registered, non-registered, others), resettlement intentions and status and age group.

Displaced Peoples' Profiles

Status of the Respondents

The samples in the survey were comprised displaced persons from registered status, non-registered status and PAB/PRE and other status. Apparently, the number of samples from registered group is the largest when comparing to other group. In Ban Tham Hin temporary shelter, the samples having registered status account for 54 % while samples from PAB/PRE/Other status account for 36 %. From the samples, non-registered people account for 10 %.

In Ban Mai Nai Soi temporary shelters, the number of samples from registered status accounts for 73 % while the second largest is the samples from non-registered group in which accounts for 17 %. The smallest is samples from PAB/PRE and other which accounts for 10 % of overall samples. In Ban Mae La temporary shelters, it is apparently seen that the samples from registered status is the largest group (56 %) while the second largest is samples from non-registered status (29 %) and it is followed by PAB/PRE/Others which accounts for 15 % (Table A.2).

Table A.2 Status of respondents in the three shelters

	Ban Tham Hin		Ban Mai Nai Soi		Ban Mae La	
	Number	Percent (%)	Number	Percent (%)	Number	Percent (%)
Registered	60	54.1	74	73.3	124	55.9
Non-registered	11	9.9	17	16.8	64	28.8
PAB/PRE/others	40	36.0	10	9.9	34	15.3
Total	111	100	101	100	222	100

Source Survey data

Gender

In Ban Tham Hin temporary shelters and Ban Mae La temporary shelters, the number of women is considerably larger than men. In Ban Tham Hin, female respondents account for 59 % while male respondents account for 41 %. Ban Mae La temporary shelters, female respondents account for 56 % of overall respondents in Ban Mae La location while male respondents account for 44 %.

In Ban Mai Nai Soi, the number of male respondents is larger than female respondents. The male respondents account for 56 % while female respondents account for 44 % (Table A.3).

Age

In Ban Tham Hin, respondents aged between 20- and 29-years old account for 36 %. The respondents at age between 30- and 39-years old account for 24 %. The respondents aged 50 years or more account for 14 % and the respondents at age between 40- and 49-years old account for 20 % while the respondents at age lower than 20 years old account for 5 %.

In Ban Mai Nai Soi, most of respondents at age between 20- and 29-years old account for 33 %. The respondents at age between 30- and 39-years old account for 25 %. The respondents at age between 40- and 49-years old account for 19 % and the respondents at age 50-years old through the highest account for 15 % while the respondents at age lower than 20-years old account for 8 %.

In Ban Mae La, most of respondents at age between 20- and 29-years old account for 31 %. The respondents at age between 30- and 39-years old account for 29 %. The respondents at age between 40- and 49-years old account for 20 % and the respondents at age 50-years old through the highest account for 12 % while the respondents at age lower than 20-years old account for 8 % (Table A.4).

Table A.3 Gender distribution in the three shelters

	Ban Tham Hin		Ban Mai Nai Soi		Ban Mae La	
	Number	Percent (%)	Number	Percent (%)	Number	Percent (%)
Female	66	59.5	45	43.7	125	56.1
Male	45	40.5	58	56.3	98	43.9
Total	111	100	103	100	223	100

Source Survey data

Table A.4 Age distribution in the three shelters

	Tham Hin		Ban Mai Nai Soi		Ban Mae La	
	Number	Percent (%)	Number	Percent (%)	Number	Percent (%)
Less than 20-years old	6	5.4	8	7.8	18	8.1
20–29-years old	40	36.0	34	33.0	69	30.9
30–39-years old	27	24.3	26	25.2	64	28.7
40–49-years old	22	19.8	20	19.4	45	20.2
50-years old and up	16	14.4	15	14.6	27	12.1
Total	111	100	103	100	223	100

Source Survey data

Marital Status

Regarding to the marital status of the respondents, it found that most of respondents had married status. In Ban Tham Hin temporary shelter, the respondents having married status account for 67 % while the second largest group is the respondents from single status (22 %). They are followed by respondents from divorced/separated status (6 %), widowed status (5 %) and other (1 %), respectively.

In Ban Mai Nai Soi, the number of respondents from married status accounts for 73 % while the number of respondents from single status accounts for 21 %. They are followed by respondents from divorced/separated status in which account for 5 % and widowed status in which account for 1 %, respectively.

In Ban Mae La, the number of respondents from married status account for 67 % while the respondents from single status account for 20 %. They are followed by respondents from widowed status in which account for 9 % and respondents from divorced and separated in which account for 3 %, respectively (Table A.5).

Table A.5 Marital status in the three shelters

	Ban Tham Hin		Ban Mai Nai Soi		Ban Mae La	
	Number	Percent (%)	Number	Percent (%)	Number	Percent (%)
Single	24	21.6	22	21.4	45	20.2
Married	74	66.7	75	72.8	150	67.3
Widowed	5	4.5	1	1.0	21	9.4
Divorced/Separated	7	6.3	5	4.9	7	3.1
Other	1	0.9	–	–	–	–
Total	111	100	103	100	223	100

Source Survey data

Ethnicity

In Ban Tham Hin temporary shelters, it is apparently seen that the largest group of respondents is Karen (S'gaw), accounting for 80 %. Karen (Pwo) account for 19 % while Karenni and Pa-o account for 1 %.

In Ban Mai Nai Soi the majority group of displaced persons is Karenni. According to the survey, the Karenni account for 87 % while Burmese account for (3 %). Shan, Burmese and other account for another 3 %.

In Ban Mae La, the Karen (S'gaw) form the majority group. It was found that 63 % of the respondents are Karen (S'gaw) while 17 % belong to the Karen (Pwo). Some 44 % of the respondents were born in other locations and 4.5 % of the respondents did not know their ethnicity (Table A.6).

Birthplace

In Ban Tham Hin, most of respondents were born in Thanithay/Tavoy state (79 %) while the second largest group was born in other locations (14 %). The samples were born in Karen state accounts for 6 %.

In Ban Mai Nai Soi, 40 % of the respondents were born in Kayah state while 38 % were born in Karen State. Seventeen percent of respondents were born in other locations and 5 % of the respondents were born in Shan state.

In Ban Mae La, 73 % of the respondents were born in Karen state while 18 % of respondents were born in other locations. Four percent of the respondents were born in the shelter while the respondents who were born in Thanithay/Tavoy state account for 1 %. The respondents who were born in Mon state accounts for 1 %. The respondents who were born in Kayah state account for 0.5 %. The respondents who were born in Shan state accounts for 0.5 % (Table A.7).

Table A.6 Respondents' ethnicity in the three shelters

	Ban Tham Hin		Ban Mai Nai Soi		Ban Mae La	
	Number	Percent (%)	Number	Percent (%)	Number	Percent (%)
Karen (Pwo)	21	18.9	1	1.0	38	17.0
Karen (S'gaw)	89	80.2	1	1.0	141	63.2
Karenni	–	–	90	87.4	7	3.1
Kachin	–	–	1	1.0	3	1.4
Mon	–	–	1	1.0	1	0.5
Pa-o	1	0.9			2	0.9
Burmese	–	–	3	2.9	9	4.0
Arakan	–	–	–	–	1	0.5
Shan	–	–	3	2.9	–	–
Other	–	–	3	2.9	11	4.9
Unknown	–	–	–	–	10	4.5
Total	111	100	103	100	223	100

Source Survey data

Table A.7 Respondents' birthplace in the three shelters

	Ban Tham Hin		Ban Mai Nai Soi		Ban Mae La	
	Number	Percent (%)	Number	Percent (%)	Number	Percent (%)
Karen state	7	6.3	39	37.9	163	73.1
Kayah state	–	–	41	39.8	1	0.5
Thanithayi / Tavoy state	88	79.3	–	–	3	1.4
Shan state	–	–	5	4.9	1	0.5
Mon state	–	–	–	–	2	0.9
Kachin state	–	–	–	–	3	1.4
Temporary shelters	–	–	–	–	9	4.0
Other	16	14.4	18	17.5	41	18.4
Total	111	100	103	100	223	100

Source Survey data

Religion

Most of respondents in Ban Tham Hin temporary shelter are Christian. Christians account for 92 % of overall respondents of this location while the second largest are the Buddhist, who account for 7 % and 1 % belong to the animist.

In Ban Mai Nai Soi, 38 % of the respondents are Christians while 36 % of the samples are the animist. The Buddhist account for 24 % and are followed by Muslims who account for 1 %. The samples with no religion account for 1 % in this location (Table A.8).

Educational Background

In Ban Tham Hin temporary shelter, 33 % of the samples graduated primary school in Myanmar while 23 % of the samples have never attended school neither in Myanmar nor in the shelter. Fourteen percent of the samples graduated middle

Table A.8 Respondents' religion in the three shelters

	Ban Tham Hin		Ban Mai Nai Soi		Ban Mae La	
	Number	Percent (%)	Number	Percent (%)	Number	Percent (%)
Animist	1	0.9	37	35.9	–	–
Buddhist	8	7.2	25	24.3	106	47.5
Christian	102	91.9	39	37.9	110	49.3
Muslim	–	–	1	1.0	7	3.1
No religion	–	–	1	1.0	–	–
Total	111	100	103	100	223	100

Source Survey data

school in Myanmar. It found that 7 % of the samplings graduated secondary school in the temporary shelters. Six percent of the samples graduated Post-10 course while 5 % of the samples graduated High school in Myanmar. It is about 4 % of the samples that graduated college/university while the samples who graduated primary school in temporary shelter account for 3 %. The samples graduated non-formal education account for 2 %. The percent as mentioned is the same as the percent of the samples who graduated other education background.

In Ban Mai Nai Soi, it found that most of the samples have never attended school neither in Myanmar nor in the temporary shelters (45 %). The samples graduated secondary school in the temporary shelters account for 13 % while the samples graduated primary school in the temporary shelter account for 10 %. The samples graduated middle school in Myanmar account for 8 %. It is rarely to gain the samples graduated high school or post-10 course; the percent of these two groups accounts for 5 % each.

In Ban Mae La, 31 % of the samples have never attended school neither in Myanmar nor in temporary shelters while the second largest is the samples graduated primary school in Myanmar in which account for 17.5 %. Fifteen percent of the samples graduated secondary school in temporary shelters whereas 12 % belong to the samples graduated high school in Myanmar and another 12 % belong to the samples graduated middle school in Myanmar. Eight percent of the samples graduated primary school in the temporary shelter. The samples graduated college/university account for 2 % while the samplings graduated post-10 course account for 2 %. The other education background accounts for 1 % of the samples in this location.

The survey points out that generally speaking, most of displaced persons in three temporary shelters have low education background. Most of them are the displaced persons with non-education and the displaced persons having primary education. It rarely found the displaced persons earning college/university education or non-formal education in these shelters (Table A.9).

Table A.9 Respondents' educational background in the three shelters

	Ban Tham Hin		Ban Mai Nai Soi		Ban Mae La	
	Number	Percent (%)	Number	Percent (%)	Number	Percent (%)
Never attended school	26	23.4	46	44.7	69	30.9
Primary school in Myanmar	37	33.3	16	15.5	39	17.5
Middle school in Myanmar	16	14.4	8	7.8	26	11.7
High school in Myanmar	6	5.4	5	4.9	27	12.1
Primary school in the temporary shelter	3	2.7	10	9.7	17	7.6
Secondary school in the temporary shelter	8	7.2	13	12.6	33	14.8
Post-10 course	7	6.3	5	4.9	4	1.8
College/university	4	3.6	–	–	5	2.2
Non-formal education	2	1.8	–	–	–	–
Other	2	1.8	–	–	3	1.4
Total	111	100	103	100	223	100

Source Survey data

Occupation

In Ban Tham Hin, it is apparently seen that most of the samples are the unemployed people (48 %). The samples who are the employed people account for 42 %. Six percent belong to self-employed people and 4 % are students.

In Ban Mai Nai Soi, 49 % of the samples are employed people while the unemployed people account for 36 %. Self-employed people and students account for 10 and 6 %, respectively.

In Ban Mae La, 49 % of the samples are unemployed people while 31 % are the employed people. Self-employed people and students account for 13 and 8 %, respectively (Table A.10).

Length of Stay

In Ban Tham Hin, most of respondents have resided in Tham Hin shelter for more than 10 years herein it accounting for 49 %. There are about 29 % of respondents that have resided in this shelter for 1–5 years and there are about 13 % of the respondents that have resided in this shelter for 6–10 years. There are about 10 % of the respondents that have resided in this shelter for less than 1 year.

In Ban Mai Nai Soi, most of respondents have resided in Ban Mai Nai Soi shelter for more than 10 years herein it accounting for 65 %. There are about 20 % of respondents that have resided in this shelter for 6–10 years and there are about 8 % of the respondents that have resided in this shelter for 1–5 years. There are about 8 % of the respondents that have resided in this shelter for less than 1 year.

In Ban Mae La, most of respondents have resided in Ban Mae La shelter for more than 10 years (40 %). There are also about 40 % of respondents that have resided in this shelter for 1–5 years and there are about 14 % of the respondents that have resided in this shelter for 6–10 years. There are about 2 % of the respondents that have resided in this shelter for less than 1 year (Table A.11).

Table A.10 Respondents' current or last occupation

	Ban Tham Hin		Ban Mai Nai Soi		Ban Mae La	
	Number	Percent (%)	Number	Percent (%)	Number	Percent (%)
Employed	47	42.3	50	48.5	68	30.6
Self-employed	7	6.3	10	9.7	28	12.6
Unemployed	53	47.8	37	35.9	109	49.1
Student	4	3.6	6	5.8	17	7.7
Total	111	100	103	100	222	100

Source Survey data

Table A.11 Respondents' length of stay in the three shelters

	Shelter					
	Tham Hin		Ban Mai Nai Soi		Ban Mae La	
	Number	Percent (%)	Number	Percent (%)	Number	Percent (%)
Less than 1 year	11	9.9	8	7.8	15	6.8
1–5 years	32	28.8	8	7.8	89	40.1
6–10 years	14	12.6	20	19.6	30	13.5
More than 10 years	54	48.6	66	64.7	88	39.6
Total	111	100	102	100	222	100

Source Survey data

Table A.12 Household size in the three shelters

	Ban Tham Hin		Ban Mai Nai Soi		Ban Mae La	
	Number	Percent (%)	Number	Percent (%)	Number	Percent (%)
1–2 persons	12	10.8	11	10.7	20	9.0
3–5 persons	49	44.1	54	52.4	91	40.8
6–10 persons	45	40.5	38	36.9	103	46.2
More than 10 persons	5	4.5	–	–	9	4.0
Total	111	100	103	100	223	100

Source Survey data

Household Size

In Ban Tham Hin, the survey found that the respondents having 3–5 family members account for 44 % while the respondents having 6–10 family members account for 41 %. The respondents having 1–2 family members account for 11 % while the respondents having more than 10 family members account for 4.5 %.

In Ban Mai Nai Soi, the survey found that the respondents having 3–5 family members account for 52 % while the respondents having 6–10 family members account for 37 %. The respondents having 1–2 family members account for 11 %.

In Ban Mae La temporary shelters, the survey found that the respondents having 6–10 family members account for 46 % while the respondents having 3–5 family members account for 41 %. The respondents having 1–2 family members account for 9 % while the respondents having more than 10 family members account for 4 % (Table A.12).

Appendix B: Focus Group Activity with Local Communities Surrounding Ban Mai Nai Soi Temporary Shelter

On Wednesday, 11th August 2010 at 9:30–12:00 o'clock at Wat Ban Nai Soi, Moo 4, Bang Moo District, Amphur Muang, Mae Hong Son Province

Participants of the focus group

1. Knowledgeable persons
2. Deputy Chief Executive of the Pang Moo Subdistrict Administrative Organisation
3. Village Chief
4. Village Chief
5. Assistant to Senior Administrator
6. Assistant to Village Chief (Security Division)
7. Assistant to Senior Administrator
8. Assistant to Village Chief (Security Division)
9. Assistant to Senior Administrator
10. Village Committee
11. Assistant to Senior Administrator
12. Assistant to Village Chief (Security Division).

Interviewees of an In-depth Interview

1. Assistant District Officer to Chief of the Administrative Operation Group, Hong Son District Office, Mae Hong Son Province	On Monday, 9th August 2010
2. International Rescue Committee's (IRC) Staff	On Tuesday, 10th August 2010
3. Senior Expert in Human Resources to the Executive Officer of Human Resource Group, Mae Hong Son Office	On Wednesday, 11th August 2010

S. Thadaniti and S. Chantavanich (eds.), *The Impact of Displaced People's Temporary Shelters on Their Surrounding Environment*, SpringerBriefs in Environment, Security, Development and Peace 16, DOI: 10.1007/978-3-319-02842-2,

Generality of Ban Mai Nai Soi Temporary Shelter

Totaling 1,600 Rais, Ban Mai Nai Soi temporary shelter is located on the upstream of Soi River. Regarding its upriver location, there is a scramble for natural resources between the displaced people and local Thai people. Originally, displaced people lived scatteringly in Mae Hong Son District. The temporary shelter was formed in 2003.

Displaced people together with temporary shelter are under administration of the district officers. Additionally, there are currently 50–60 Thai Volunteer Militiamen (OrSor) looking after the displaced people around the shelter as well.

Generally, displaced people in the temporary shelter live on the charity of TBBC who provides livelihood assistance such as construction materials and monthly food rations. Dried food rations supplied are dried chilies, iodised salt and rotten bean, etc.

There is no contradictory between displaced people and local Thai communities in Ban Mai Nai Soi area because both groups of people are related in kindred.

A discussion on the focus group was conducted to acknowledge any issues of the environmental impacts. The impacts include both positive and negative impacts of the district of Bang Moo village—located near Ban Mai Nai Soi temporary shelter. In addition, the issue on the relationship between the displaced people and the local Thai communities living around the shelter was also taken into account. Finally, any suggestions on the remedy and collaboration of the organisations involved were also discussed. A conclusion details as follows.

Problematic Issues

Homeland Security Issue

Problem of the Entrance/Exit to the Temporary Shelter

There is no regulation and time restriction in regards to getting in and going out of people in the shelter. At present, there is a shared responsibility of various authorities such as the military and the Thai Volunteer Militia (OrSor) to monitor the shelter. For instant, the military helps to guard against the border and the Thai Volunteer Militia (OrSor) takes charge of the local administration. However, the OrSor could not cover internal security to all local areas because the shelter's area is too big and the displaced people have high population density. The checkpoint station of the passing or coming of all vehicles takes place only at the gateway of the temporary shelter. A motorcycle becomes a popular means of travelling for people in the shelter who prefer to commute from one place to another by a shorter route. The shorter route has both advantages and disadvantages. On one hand, the shorter route is more convenient to access and sometimes, can even exempt from the checkpoint station. On the other hand, the shorter route is a risky area for crime and violation of law such as distribution of narcotics, i.e. methamphetamine pills, crystal methamphetamine hydrochloride and all kinds of drugs spreading; illegal labor employment; encroachment on forests and deforestation, etc. The shorter route is the risky area due to its easy accessibility and connection that helps to facilitate communication between the underhanded businessmen and the displaced people. Thus, the shorter route becomes a big concerned on any damages caused by the authorities and organisations involved and the temporary shelter. Therefore, all responsible organisations should provide guidance as well as set up regulation enforcement in the shelter.

Incomprehensive on the Regulations and Law of Thailand

There are hundreds of motorcycles in the shelter, as the traders sell motorcycles to the displaced people by using someone' else name. Inevitably, the more motorcycles use, the more accidents occur because the displaced people do not know Thai traffic rules.

Language and Communication Problem

Karen language is the primary language for communication of the displaced people in the temporary shelter. Meanwhile, English language is used as a medium of instruction at school. English language is a common language used at school because most of the educational assistance is from the international non-governmental organisations. Consequently, displaced students are not fluent in Thai language, especially speaking and reading. Due to low proficient communication skill in Thai language, the displaced people are not able to understand Thai law in regards to the motorcycle riding rules. This leads to a lot of motorcycle accidents in Pang Moo district. For example, often time there is an accident of motorcycle crashing victim's children.

Natural Resources Security Issue

Problem of Water Resources

Ban Mai Nai Soi temporary shelter is located on Nai Soi preserved forest. On the right hand side is the Pai forest river conservation. Pai river is an essential fountainhead of Huay Nam Soi creek. Water resources from Huay Nam Soi creek is used to nourish displaced people and local Thai communities in Pang Moo area. While water in Huay Nam Soi creek flows from the north, water in Huay Pong creek runs through the shelter from the south. Water resources from both Huay

Nam Soi and Huay Pong creeks converge at Ban Sob Soi (Moo 8) in the area of Pang Moo district. This waterway is called Pai River which is the main river of Mae Hon Son province. Since the temporary shelter is located on the fountainhead of the river, the problem of water resources takes place as follows.

Problem of the Competition Over Water Supply

Ban Mai Nai Soi temporary shelter is located on the preserved forest, an area of the essential fountainhead. This fountainhead is the important water resource for consumption of local communities in Pang Moo district. Regarding the shelter's area located nearby the source of water together with overcrowded population in the shelter, the competition on water resources between the local communities and the displaced people is inevitable, as all users use the same source of water for consumption.

Generally, water is a particular problem in dry season every year. During this time of the year, there is an inadequate water supply for agriculture needs, as the displaced people store water from the creek for their owns consumption. In this regards, UNDP provides funding assistant for the amount of 1,500,000 Baht on the highland waterworks project to help local communities in Ban Nai Soi (Moo 4) to solve the problem of water scarcity. This aid is a pilot project set up to reduce bias between the local communities around the shelter and the displaced people.

Problem of Wastewater Disposal

IRC is responsible for water management and supply system in Ban Mai Nai Soi temporary shelter. To do so, water is pumped up from the creek and stored in a water tank with chloride added. Then, water transmission pipeline will be installed from the water tank to the distribution point in order to let the water transfer to each household in the shelter. By this way, the residents will have clean water for consumption. Remarkably, the IRC supplies only clean water without setting up any household wastewater management system. What the displaced people usually do is to let wastewater run along a small water course. The used water together with swill and garbage are stored in the water course. When the rainy season comes, all the waste will run off to the creek. As a result, people who live in the local communities around the shelter get dirty water, as it contaminates with the waste.

Not Appreciated Things Received

The international organisations namely, UN, UNDP or private organisations try to organise a fundraising project to gather contributions from both private and public sectors as well as from the international organisations to support humanitarian assistance to the displaced people in the shelter. These kinds of assistances get approval from the local communities. However, there is a failure in the internal rules and regulations. The displaced people take all the donated items for granted by selling them to someone else. The items received are rice, supplement nutrition food, charcoal, cooking oil and vegetable. Even the donated cloth will be sold to local Thai people at a cheaper price. Then, they will spend the money earned to buy something else instead.

Usually, the displaced people like to put charcoal and iodised salt up for sale. When the charcoal is sold, they don't have it for household consumption. This leads to a problem of illegal logging to produce firewood. The process of deforestation is done by two ways. The first method is called 'Garn Mai'. The hardwood trees are killed by chopping its trunk all the way to the heartwood and leaving it for a week to let all the leaves dry out and die. The second method is called 'Gan Mai'. The trees are killed by drilling a hole on the trunk and putting some chemical powder inside the hole to let the tree die down.

In respect of bamboo depletion, displaced people use bamboo for housing construction and home repair. Furthermore, they cut bamboo from the local forest to make bamboo panel or basket for sale. This problem can cause a huge environmental damage if there is no strict rule enforcement as far as the birth rate of the displaced people is concerned. Ban Mai Nai Soi is a big temporary shelter due to its high population density and birth rate. The birth rate is up to a ratio of 50–60 infants per month. This number is higher than the local communities' birth rate. The high birth rate together with overcrowded population will lead to the future problem of deforestation. Therefore, there should be a strictly regulation to control the displaced people to enforce the rule.

Problem of Energy

In Ban Mai Nai Soi, battery, candles and kerosene lamps are used as a source of power for lighting and monthly charcoal rations are used for cooking. Problem occurs when the displaced people always sell charcoal to the local Thai traders. Therefore, they do not have sufficient charcoal for household consumption. Thus, the displaced people conduct the illegal logging inside the local forest to produce firewood. Apparently, this energy problem leads to a problem of deforestation in the preserved forest area.

Problem of a Reduction in Biological Diversity

Nai Soi national preserved forest is abundant of various forest resources and wildlife. Tong Teung plant (local northern plant), bamboo and wildlife are the crucial resources for livelihood and economy in this area. In this regard, there is a competition for natural resources between the local people living around the temporary shelter and the displaced people.

Tong Teung plant is an essential plant for livelihood and economy of both displaced people and local people surrounding the shelter. These two groups of people have similar needs of Tong Teung leaves for home building and maintenance as well as for sale. However, both groups of people have different ways of picking up the leaves. On one hand, local people usually pick up the leaves during fall. On the other hand, displaced people use 'Gan Mai' method to accelerate the plant to dry out faster so that they could collect the leaves as often as they prefer. Apart from the household used, displaced people are able to sell Tong Teung leaves to TBBC in the shelter. The buying and selling transaction between the displaced people and the TBBC is a kind of insider trading. As a consequence, the Tong Teung plants are not sufficient for local people surrounding the shelter due to its depletion by the displaced people.

Bamboo is being cut illegally from the local forest by the displaced people to use for home construction and repair. In addition, they also use some part of the bamboo to weave home appliance for household use and for sale. Even worst, besides an illegal bamboo logging, the displaced people also cut bamboo shoot which will stop the bamboo from growing and propagation. Thus, an illegal bamboo and bamboo shoot cutting cause a rapid reduction of bamboo trees. As a matter of facts, its reduction is faster than the other trees in the Nai Soi national preserved forest.

The major cause of a reduction in Tong Teung plant and bamboo trees in the Nai Soi national preserved forest comes from an internal purchasing order from the TBBC. Since the trade is being done internally, the local people lose their income, as they do not know when the buying and selling taking place.

Pertaining to wildlife in the Nai Soi national preserved forest, there are currently extinction of some animal species such as hornbill and armadillo. These two species have already disappeared from the forest. Nevertheless, some species have only a few numbers left such as topknot bulbul or so-called 'Nok Pik Ja Noy' by the local people. The cause of extinction and a reduction of some animal species come from the displaced people's hunting wildlife for food. As a result, the local people surrounding the shelter lack source of food and income. This encourages the local people to develop bad attitude towards the displaced people.

Other Problems

The establishment of Ban Mai Nai Soi temporary shelter does not only cause environmental impacts, but create security issues to the local people as well. Since the areas of Ban Mai Nai Soi temporary shelter and local Thai communities are located next to each other, the accessibility and communication between two groups of people are very easy, leading to the following problems.

Motorcycle Problem

At present, the motorcycle business between the trader and the displaced people in the shelter is very easy. That is, the displaced people buy a motorcycle under the name of their Thai acquaintance, when the trader delivers the motorcycle to them in the shelter. Consequently, there are several hundred motorcycles in the shelter.

Birth Rate Problem

Ban Mai Nai Soi temporary shelter is home to many displaced persons fleeing fighting in Myanmar. Inevitably, the overcrowded population leads to a problem of high birth rate. The birth rate ratio in the shelter is 50–60 infants per month. This number is higher than the infant's birth rate of the whole Pang Moo district. An overwhelming population generates new problems of deforestation and natural resources depletion.

Permanent Construction Problem

With the purpose to ensure certainty to the displaced people, the non-governmental organisations have set up their office, medical center and various public utilities inside the shelter to provide all kinds of assistance needed. The construction of public facilities and utilities causes some tensions to the local Thai people. As they perceive that all the construction buildings is not just for a temporary purpose, but they will be a permanent resident for the displaced people. The local people's concern is that all the existing problems caused by the displaced people will remain unsolved.

Security Problem

Ban Mai Nai Soi temporary shelter is located about 5–8 km away from Myanmar boundary. According to geographical features of Pang Moo district, Ban Mai Sa Pae village (Moo 9) has the most nearest location from Myanmar border. Due to its proximity to the border, this village is vulnerable when there is a fight between Myanmar force and the ethnic minority groups. The local people in this area get scare of the battle impact from the neighboring country in regards to harm that may happen to them by incident. As far as life safety is concerned, it is found that the armed ethnic groups could access to and go back and forth to Ban Mai Sa Pae village several occasions. There was an incident of the local Thai people, living in Ban Doi Saeng (Moo 13), who lost his legs in bomb blast from a battle along Myanmar border.

Problem Caused by Employees of the Non-Governmental Organisations

Often time, the drivers of the non-governmental organisations make trouble to the local people surrounding the shelter. For instance, the drivers drive too fast and cause an accident. Particularly, when there is a transportation of goods to the shelter, the pick-up drivers do not have a regular driving schedule. This, in turn, interferes with local people's lives. There is a case of serious damage at Pang Moo district caused by the drivers who got drunk and cut the power line.

Problem of the Negative Attitude of Local People Surrounding the Shelter Towards the Displaced People

While various relief agencies including government sectors, international organisations and private organisations pay attention to aid displaced people, the local people surrounding the shelter who have a rudiment living condition are in trouble and being neglected by the aforementioned organisations.

Despite of the living condition, the local people also encounter economic crisis for the following causes: Local people become unemployed, as the NGO will not hire them, but hire the displaced people to work instead. The bidding project on bamboo and Tong Teung leaves does not give any chances to the local people to participate in the competition. There is also no public announcement on the bidding. The TBBC just purchases bamboo and Tong Teung leaves cheaply from the displaced people. Besides, the local people and the displaced people do compete with each other to collect Tong Teung leaves. Generally, the displaced people pick up the leaves before the local people do.

Problem of Garbage Management in the Temporary Shelter

Garbage in the shelter will be divided into three categories as follows:

(1) General garbage: The pick-up date is on every Friday. The IRC has arranged one truck to collect garbage from 30 garbage collection stations. The total amount of garbage pick-up is around one ton. All these garbage will be incinerated by using tire as a burning fuel. Nowadays, burning oil is used instead. Burning smoke and dust is floating in the atmosphere depending on wind direction.
With the habit of dumping the garbage without sorting, COERR collaborates with IRC to teach the displaced people to sort garbage and waste so that they know which one can be recycled or sold to the COERR. COERR will buy the garbage on every Saturday and Sunday.
(2) Hazardous waste from the medical center
The hazardous waste will be collected every Friday. This particular garbage will be disposed in the clinic's incinerator.
(3) Battery
The battery disposal site consists of four concrete pipes. When the first pipe is filled up, it will be closed by the concrete lid. Then, the second pipe will be opened up for disposal.

Other Problems in the Shelter

(1) An increasing number of the displaced people in the shelter
NGO's assistant together with public road construction project becomes a major factor, inducing the influx of displaced people to escape the politic upheaval in Myanmar to Thailand. In 2009, the district office started the project on public road construction. The construction started from the local Thai village unit to the temporary shelter.

(2) Shortage of skilled labor
Many displaced people who were resettled to a third country are skilled laborers including teachers or doctors. The remaining displaced people are unskilled workers who rely solely on NGO assistance.

The Positive Impacts

(1) Cheap labor: Local people are satisfied that there are displaced people living nearby the community. The displaced people do not only serve as a source of seasonal laborers for their field, they are also a source of cheap laborers.

(2) Low impacts on local communities surrounding the shelter: In 2009, UNDP carried out many community development programs to support livelihood improvement of local people living around Ban Nai Soi shelter, Muang district, Mae Hon Son province. The development programs emphasise on local participation. The distribution of grants is also provided to support the development projects and also to help those villagers affected by the displaced people in the shelter. Since there is insufficient water supple in the village, the project on "water for a better quality of life" is implemented. To further this, irrigation ditch is built to reserve water at Huay Sai creek. There is another project worth 1.6 million baht on "the development/expansion of the highland water system with its water filter tank". The contribution is also given to Rom Graw Pang Tong School; this school is under the royal patronage. Also, the school camp on the agricultural project named "Let's learn a pathway to self-sufficient" is held for the purpose of practicing agricultural skills in school.

The Negative Impacts

(1) Deforestation: This problem leads to another issue of a scarcity of food resources of the local people. The findings from the survey of the village leader and villagers in Moo 13, Ban Doi Saeng reveal that in 1994–1997, some wild animals such as hornbill and pangolin were disappeared. In 1997–2002, the forest was reclaimed for planting vegetables, chilies and rice. An invader intruded into the National wildlife conservation park. Some wild animals such as barking deer and wild boar together with Tong Kor plant (similar features to Tong Teung plant, but have bigger leaves) started decreasing in number. In 2002–present, forest land and wildlife still have been intruded. There is an increasing deforestation and some wild animals begin to extinct as the displaced people kill them for food.

(2) Thievery problem in the local community: Field crop and homegrown produce are stolen.
(3) Local people are in trouble from the impact of battling between Myanmar military government and the ethnic minorities along the border: The villagers lost their legs from bomb. The NGO supplied rice to the injured people in order to soothe them.

Guideline Solutions between Local People Surrounding the Shelter and Displaced People

1. Create understanding between local people and displaced people to lessen bias. At present, there are the activities on sport competition between these two groups of people, reforestation project on the collaboration of both local people and displaced people and hire of service from the displaced people to plant trees.
2. Limited authority of the Chief Executive of the Subdistrict Administrative Organisation to take action. The Chief Executive of the SAO does not have the authority to take care of or control the displaced people in the temporary shelter. This duty belongs to the District Chief Officer. Therefore, when there is trouble, the Chief Executive of the SAO can only listen to the problem and bring that particular problem to the meeting. Thus, the best solution for this problem is to have both groups of people communicate with each other whenever there is a problem. The local community should be able to take care of or control the displaced people in the shelter.
3. Pay attention to the local Thai people. The non-governmental organisations that are responsible for the shelter should make some contribution to the local Thai people living around the shelter. NGO's support or assistance to the local people will create good feeling to each other.

Appendix C: Focus Group Activity with the Local Community Surrounding the Ban Mae La Temporary Shelter

On Friday, 3rd September 2010 at 13:30–16:00 o'clock at Ban Ok Pha Ru Moo 3, Mae La district, Amphur Tha Song Yang, Tak province

Participants of the Focus Group

1. Assistant to Village Chief (Security Division)
2. Member of the Subdistrict Administrative Organisation
3. Assistant to Village Chief
4. Member of the Subdistrict Administrative Organisation
5. Assistant to Village Chief
6. Village Committee
7. Village Chief
8. Assistant to Agricultural Scholar
9. Chief Administrator of the Subdistrict Administrative Organisation
10. Assistant to Mae La SAO Clerk.

Interviewees of an In-depth Interview

1. Public Health Specialist (Assistant to Public Health), Amphur Tha Song Yang, Tak province	On Friday, 3rd September 2010
2. Academic Public Health Specialist (Amphur Tha Song Yang Public Health) Tak province	On Friday, 3rd September 2010
3. Ban Mae La Chief Executive of the SAO 4. Ban Mae La Chief Administrator of the SAO (Finance section)	On Friday, 3rd September 2010

S. Thadaniti and S. Chantavanich (eds.), *The Impact of Displaced People's Temporary Shelters on Their Surrounding Environment*, SpringerBriefs in Environment, Security, Development and Peace 16, DOI: 10.1007/978-3-319-02842-2,

Perspective on positive/negative environmental impacts of Ban Mae La temporary shelter on local communities surrounding the shelter is as follows.

Negative Impacts

Natural Resources

Forest

Originally, the area of the temporary shelter used to be very fertile. The establishment of the temporary shelter as well as the influx of the displaced people in the shelter leads to deforestation. The displaced people reclaim forest for agriculture and home construction. Noticeably, the house's stilts of the displaced people who have been living in the shelters for more than 5 years are made of teak wood. Besides depleting local forests for housing construction, the displaced people also cut trees down to make charcoal or even transform wood and transport it out of the shelter to be sold somewhere else. The wood cutting machine used is portable panel saw which is quite and takes only 30 min to cut one tree. Yet, the problem of deforestation has been minimised since NGOs supplies Eucalyptus poles to the displaced people.

Prevention guideline (*remedy planning*): The local community provides a guideline to solve this problem by having the District Chief Officer together with Chief Executive of the SAO make a mutual agreement on the community forest area. The agreement clearly specifies which area is for land usage. There will also be an inspection twice a month.

Water Resources

Problem of Dirty Water

Formerly, Mei River and Huay Ok Pha Ru creek used to be sources of water for the local community. Currently, these water resources are being polluted, as the rivers are contaminated with germ and garbage. A needle from clinic or illegal drugstore is contaminated with wastewater and flew into the river. Thus, many local people who drink water from these rivers get sick of Cholera disease. Due to people's illness, the Tha Song Yang public health make an announcement to prohibit people to use water or collect vegetables from these rivers.

Water Resources

Local people do not have enough water for consumption, as the displaced people sell water out. Thus, the Chief Executive of the SAO and the Solidarity's International have discussed about building an irrigation weir to keep water for dry season.

Garbage

Ten years ago, garbage at the temporary shelter will be disposed by incinerating in front of the shelter area. Later, COERR took responsibility for the management of the garbage disposal in the shelter by providing garbage disposal stations and the garbage wells. Since there is too much garbage, the garbage management system is not thoroughly worked. Some waste is contaminated with water, running out of the shelter. This causes agricultural damages to local people.

Aquatic Animals

Formerly, Mei River was full of shells. The amount was too much that there was no room to walk. Since the establishment of the temporary shelter, those shells are now extinct.

Security

Stealing

(1) The displaced people sneak out of the shelter to steal corn or fish for their own consumption and for resell.
(2) Tong Teung leaves are stolen for home construction or for resell. Generally, Tong Teung leaves fall during dry season which is a pick-up season. Yet, the displaced people, especially the Kala group, will sneak out of the shelter to collect the leaves twice a day according to an order from the merchant. The displaced people will use 'Gan Mai' method in their pick up; that is, to make the trees die first and then collect the leaves later.
    The solution guideline: The investor (bid winner) is assigned to take care of the local people surrounding the shelter. During the Tong Teung leaves' auction time, the bid winner should contribute financial support to develop the local community.

Hygiene of the Displaced People in the Temporary Shelter

Both cholera and gastrointestinal tract and its disease of the displaced people as well as the local people are infected by personal contact. That is, the infection passes from one person to another person living in the same area. The cause of infection comes from water and food of the vehicles venders rather than from the shelter itself. According to water management system in the shelter, water consumed will be mixed with soil and chlorine every week. There is also an announcement, encouraging the displaced people to drink boiled water. There are some displaced people who do not boil water; therefore, when they drink it they will smell chlorine.

Ban Mae La temporary shelter is the biggest shelter in Thailand. There are approximately 60,000 displaced people in the shelter (a reference from the Epidemiological institute). Yet, information from the public health office is different from the other institutes because each institute report different statistic.

The causes of disease are categorised by type of infection such as human, water or food and insect as follows:

(1) Gastrointestinal tract disease comes from water and food such as acute diarrhea with normal symptom and severe symptom, cholera, typhoid and dysentery, etc. Statistics from Mae Sod hospital insists that there are about 400 patients sick of cholera in this year. From the statistics, the number of displaced patients is equaled to local patients of Tak province per year. In addition, displaced patients take the second rank of the country. The first rank is Pattani province.
Information on the gastrointestinal tract disease caused by water and food is as follows:
In 2005, there was an epidemic of cholera in the temporary shelter.
In 2006, there was an epidemic of cholera in the local community caused by direct contact of people. The spreading of the disease originated from the displaced people getting out of the shelter and some local people entering into the shelter.
In 2007, there was an epidemic of cholera in the area again.
In 2009, there was the epidemic of typhoid and German measles.
In 2010, there was an epidemic of cholera in the shelter. From the investigation on water used in the shelter of the Mae Sod hospital's staff, it was found that there were Coliform bacteria contaminated in the water. Staff at Mae Sod hospital had sent the examination result to NGOs that were involved in the shelter area.
(2) An insect is an infectious disease agent of the hemorrhagic fever. The infectious agent developed from Myanmar. There were 500 displaced patients in the

shelter and 100 local patients at Tha Song Yang district. Similar to Cholera, the hemorrhagic fever take the second rank of the disease in Thailand.

(3) Disposal well causes an infection to disease. Waste disposal well causes more impacts to local people surrounding the shelter than the displaced people, as the disposal well's location is near the local community. Particularly, the waste disposal method is not a close system; thus, bacteria and germ are spreading. Furthermore, the disposal well is located near a source of water; therefore, it enables germ and bacteria to circulate out of the shelter area easily.

Problem of Hygiene in the Temporary Shelter

The unsolved problem in regards to hygiene found in the shelter is as follows:

1. Every 6 months, there will be the new NGO officers come to work at the shelter. The rotation of the newcomers affects the continuity of work. However, those who render consistent service in the shelter are the officer from Thai government.
2. The foreign specialists used to get invited to enhance knowledge to the displaced people on how to protect themselves from any diseases. This project was not workable, as the specialists invited were not proficient in the tropical diseases.
3. There was an exchange Epidemiologist from Myanmar coming to examine epidemic disease in the temporary shelter. However, the Burmese Epidemiologists did not reveal their examination result because it might have some impacts on the temporary shelter. Regarding this reason, the problem cannot be solved.

Remedy to the Hygiene Problem in the Temporary Shelter

In the past, this problem has been resolved as follows:

1. There was a pilot study initiated by the USCRI (USA Ambassador) to build a public health hospital in the temporary shelter.
2. Tha Song Yang public health carried out the "Buffer Project" to minimise the problem of disease spreading. This project had been done consecutively for many years. But this project has not been held in a recent year.
3. Problem solving in the shelter should be solved through the process of EIA and HIA simultaneously to achieve the best result.

Positive Impacts

1. Displaced people is a source of cheap laborers available for the local community to hire.
2. Bus operator and motorcycle rider earn income from public carrier such as bus operators and motorcycle riders earns their income from transportation service provided to the displaced passengers.

Negative Impacts

The negative impacts are categorised according to the following aspects.

Water Resources and Garbage

1. During dry season, the displaced people in the shelter will retain water for their own consumption, causing insufficient water for the local people.
2. Wastewater is contaminated with garbage, flowing into the agricultural area of the local people. The local people have to pick up the garbage in their rice field.

Natural resources (forest/forest produce/wildlife)

1. There is a competition on natural resources such as Tong Teung leaves, bamboo and forest produce between the displaced people and the local people. A smuggle of forest produce is done both day and night by the displaced people. Thus, local people lose their income.
2. Wild animals such as pheasant and monitor lizard have been disappeared because the displaced people hunt them for food.
   In the Tong Teung leaves' auction, the bid winners will not hire local people to work for them. Displaced people are hire to work instead. When the displaced people work in the forest, they usually steal forest produce such as bamboo shoot with them. As a result, the Chief Administrator of the Subdistrict Administrative Organisation strictly forbids people to access the forest as well as prohibits them to look for bamboo shoot in order to let the bamboo shoot grows up to bamboo tree. Any lawbreaker will be under arrested.

Other Impacts

1. The displaced people often put the donated items such as charcoal up for sale to the local people or the middleman. Consequently, the displaced people log the forest to collect timber to make charcoal for their own use.
2. Presently, most people in the shelter are Islam. They are from the other area who get into the shelter by an invitation of Islam people inside the shelter. As a consequent, there is more Islam people in the shelter than the whole local community at Mae La district.
3. The displaced people steal agriculture products such as corn. They steal it for consumption and also for resell.
4. The displaced people steal motorcycle. Although the local people know that the displaced people steal their motorcycles, they cannot take any legal action against the displaced people because there are a lot of them in the shelter.
5. Teenagers who belong to a motorcycle gangster always gather in front of the shelter.
6. There is a conflict between the displaced teenagers and Thai teenagers. The dispute between them have developed to homicide.
7. Karen soldiers ambush and shoot their gun into Thai boundary.

Appendix D: An In-depth Interview Suan Phung Subdistrict Administrative Organisation

On Thursday, 15th July 2010 at 8:30–12:00 o'clock at Suan Phung Subdistrict Administrative Organisation, Amphur Suan Phung, Ratchburi province

Chief administrator of Suan Phung Subdistrict Administrative Organisation, Amphur Suan Phung, Ratchburi province

General Information

1. Water flowing direction in Amphur Suan Phung runs from Huay Nam Sai creek to the following areas: to Huay Khun (Hub Kra Torn), to Pha Chee river, to Huay Ta Koo, to Mae Krong river and returns to Ratchburi province.
2. Population under the township is divided into 8 Moo by race as follows:

Moo 1/2/3/7/8 the Thai-Karen people
Moo 4/6 Thai people from the central area of the country(Lao–Vietnam)
Moo 5 Thai people from the central area of the country

3. The relationship between the displaced people and local Thai people is related in kinship.
4. Tham Hin temporary shelter is governed directly by the Ministry of the interior and controlled by the army engineers.

Problematic Issues

Ban Tham Hin temporary shelter is located on Tham Hin area (Moo 5), Suan Phung district, Amphur Suan Phung, Ratchburi province. Regarding its purpose of convenient control, this shelter was established in 1996 to gather all displaced people who fled from political battle in Myanmar and lived scatteredly in Suan Phung area in Thailand. The shelter later on was named "Ban Tham Hin

S. Thadaniti and S. Chantavanich (eds.), *The Impact of Displaced People's Temporary Shelters on Their Surrounding Environment*, SpringerBriefs in Environment, Security, Development and Peace 16, DOI: 10.1007/978-3-319-02842-2,

temporary shelter". Of the nine shelters in Thailand, this shelter is the nearest shelter to Bangkok. Geographically, Ban Tham Hin shelter lies in a steep sided valley with its total area of 40 Rais. It is about 10 km away from Myanmar–Thai border. The shelter is divided into four administrative zones. The four zones are close down since all Burmese students had moved out of the shelter.

Since the formation of Ban Tham Hin temporary shelter in 1996, there are more and more displaced people who suffer from political conflicts flee to Thailand. An influx leads to environmental impacts inside the shelter as well as local communities surrounding the shelter as follows:

Water Resources Problem

Lum Huay Klum creek is the most significant water resources for consumption of the displaced people. The river source located on the north of the shelter runs from Lum Huay Khun (Hub Ka Torn) to Pha CheeRiver and also flows to Ban Huay Khum area (Moo 6). The size of Lum Huay Khun creek is not big; that is, the creek does not have that much of its wide and deep. Therefore, there is always a competition on water resources between the displaced people and the local people, especially during dry season. Due to the higher population of the displaced people, they need a lot of water for consumption.

Pertaining to the problem on water competition, the Subdistrict Administrative Organisation proposed a reservoir construction project to solve the problem of water scarcity of the local people in dry season. However, this project became an abortive plan, as the area planned for reservoir construction was located near the temporary shelter.

Garbage Problem

IRC is responsible for garbage management in the shelter. The IRC has separated waste into wet garbage and general garbage. There is one big hole of wet garbage disposal site located in the back of the main office. There are also seven general garbage disposal stations scattered around the shelter. Besides, there is one incinerated garbage place located on the entrance of the shelter near the checkpoint of the Thai Volunteer Militia (OrSor).

IRC has two methods in eliminating garbage inside the shelter. Rubbish landfill dump is used for wet garbage when the hole is full. Other general garbage will be incinerated at the disposal site. However, IRC cannot dispose all the garbage in the shelter, as there is a lot of garbage left on street and some garbage in the creek flowing through the shelter.

Problem on Other Issues

Besides environmental impacts on local communities surrounding the shelter, there is a problem of stealing on the agricultural products. This generates direct impacts on local people. In the past, the displaced people used to steal agricultural products for their own consumption. Yet, nowadays, they steal frequently in a big quantity for reselling. This causes a lot of agricultural damages to local people.

Another problem is trespass to land of the underhanded investors. Since year 2007, there was a group of investors from other locality renting land from the only local people who had a receipt of the local maintenance tax in Suan Phung district to cultivate rubber trees. Since the geographical area of Suan Phung district is nestled deep in the valley, it is easy for someone to encroach on forest. In addition, there is an illegal hiring going on in the shelter. This violation leads to a problem of homeland security. It is against the law by letting displaced people leave the shelter. When there is a hiring, the displaced people have to sneak out of the shelter to work, leading to the problem of illegal laborers and security later on.

The Encroachment on Forests and the Changes in Land Usage

In the past, local people used some space in the forest for cultivation. However, a physical survey in 1992–1995 had declared the forest area as a state property. Later, an investor had encroached on forest to cultivate rubber trees. Since the geographical area of Tham Hin is nestled deep in the valley, when the land is used for rubber trees cultivation, there is more and more encroachment on forest. There is only 10 % of a legal tenant who rents land at Suan Phung district. However, the encroachment on forest has changed land use currently for cultivation to tourism.

Problem on Garbage Disposal

The IRC should separate the type of garbage disposed before landfill because the disposal hole is located near source of water.

Problem on Stealing of the Agricultural Products

Normally, it is Karen's way of living to collect forest produce or things on the sideways for their consumption. Presently, they pick up a lot of these things for resell. Thus, many agricultural products of the local people are stolen very often.

Problem solving guidelines on the environment by the Subdistrict Administrative Organisation (SAO)

a. Water resources problem: The Huay Khum reservoir construction was proposed to help local people to have sufficient water for consumption. This proposal was not approved, as the reservoir was located near the shelter.

b. Forest problem: There were many reforestation projects such as sprinkle grass seeds to let the grass cover the soil.
c. Garbage problem: To encourage awareness to the local people, the SAO provided knowledge together with financial support to manage garbage disposal in the community.
d. Other problems: The SAO suggested both UN and NGOs to take care of the local communities surrounding the shelter. For instance, when there is an epidemic, the infection is spreading to the local communities.

Appendix E: NGOs and Donor Organisations in Ban Tham Hin, Ban Mai, Nai Soi and Mae La

Below follows an overview of NGOs and donor organisations working in the three temporary shelters studies: Ban Tham Hin, Ban Mai Nai Soi and Mae La.

Ban Tham Hin Temporary Shelter

There are six NGOs working in Ban Tham Hin, three of which work in the area of environmental protection (Table 8). These are the International Refugee Committee (IRC), the Catholic Office for Emergency Relief and Refugees (COERR), and the Thai Burma Border Consortium (TBBC).

(1) IRC has the responsibility to implement the program on sanitation, environment and water management including monitoring of water quality, which has been implemented within the shelter for over 10 years. The program is a partnership with Environmental Health (EH), an agency formed by the shelter's sub-committees themselves. Details of sanitation program include maternal child health and nutrition (MCHN), clinical services, eye care project, and legal counseling services (LAC). It aims to reduce the incidence of water borne and hygiene related diseases among the displaced persons through the provision of improved potable water and sanitation systems. IRC is responsible for setting up sanitation systems, water piping networks and waste disposal and recycling campaigns.

(2) COERR is responsible for protecting the environment in the shelter's surroundings. Tham Hin suffers from severe deforestation in the area surrounding the shelter by commercial investors, making the area prone to floods and landslides. COERR promotes tree-planting activities, organic farming and the building of rocky embankments to prevent landslides.

(3) TBBC works through the Camp Committee in distributing food, shelter and non-food items such as cooking fuels, construction materials and basic livelihood tools. TBBC implements distribution services similar to other camps. The District chief joins hands with TBBC to reclaim the forest through

S. Thadaniti and S. Chantavanich (eds.), *The Impact of Displaced People's Temporary Shelters on Their Surrounding Environment*, SpringerBriefs in Environment, Security, Development and Peace 16, DOI: 10.1007/978-3-319-02842-2,

Table E.1 Lists the NGOs providing support in Ban Tham Hin temporary shelter

No.	Name of organisation	Supporting roles/responsibilities
1	Thai Burma Border Consortium (TBBC)	- Food, shelter and non-food items
2	ZOA Refugee care	- Primary and secondary education
3	Catholic Office for Emergency Relief and Refugees (COERR)	- Environmental protection activities such as tree planting, vocational training and social services to underprivileged groups
4	International Refugee Committee (IRC)	- Healthcare, drinking water and legal services
5	Shanti Volunteer Association (SVA)	- Library programs and cultural promotion activities
6	Right to Play (RTP)	- Child development through sports activities

Source The authors

planting of bamboo around the refugee camps at Tham Hin camp. Bamboo plantations not only provide building materials but also protect the land from soil erosion and provide nutritious bamboo shoots for consumption (Table E.1).

Ban Mai Nai Soi Temporary Shelter

There are seven NGOs working within the site (Table E.2). Three of these work in the field of environmental management, namely the International Refugee Committee (IRC), the Catholic Office for Emergency Relief and Refugees (COERR), and the Thai Burma Border Consortium (TBBC).

(1) IRC has the responsibility to implement the program on sanitation, environment and water management including monitoring of water quality, which has been implemented within the shelter for over 10 years. The program is a partnership with Environmental Health (EH), an agency formed by the shelter's sub-committees themselves. Details of sanitation program include maternal child health and nutrition (MCHN), clinical services, eye care project, legal counseling services (LAC). IRC is responsible for setting up sanitation systems, water piping networks and waste disposal and recycling campaigns.
(2) COERR is responsible for protecting the environment in the shelter's surroundings and has been in operation for the last 8 years. Among the environmental protection campaigns initiated within the camp are trees planting, training on how to make organic fertilisers, and seedlings distribution, all with the purpose to create awareness and sense of responsibilities among shelter populations for their surroundings. The project aims to eliminate discrimination against displaced persons as the ones causing environmental damage and create a good image for displaced persons in caring for their surroundings.

Table E.2 Lists the NGOs providing support in Ban Mai Nai Soi

No.	Name of organisation	Supporting roles/responsibilities
1	Thai Burma Border Commission (TBBC)	- Food, shelter and non-food items
2	Planned Parenthood Association of Thailand (PPAT)	- Reproductive health among DPs
3	Karenni Refugee Committees (KnRC)	- Community based Organisations (CBO) that became the Refugees Committee in managing the camp as well as being the focal point in coordination with NGOs. KNRC is based in Mae Hong Son
4	Catholic Office for Emergency Relief and Refugees (COERR)	- Environmental protection activities such as tree planting, vocational training and social services to underprivileged groups
5	Women's Education for Advancement and Empowerment (WEAVE)	- Set up of early Child development centers (with 133 volunteers and 1793 children under care). Women's education
6	Ruam Mit Foundation for the youths (DARE)	- Campaigns against drugs, alcohol and HIV/AIDS
7	International Refugee Committee (IRC)	- Health care, drinking water and legal services

Source The authors

Additionally, COERR implements other social services for the handicapped and the underprivileged through the provision of educational and sport resources, teaching materials, vocational programs like soap, shampoo and candle making, sewing, agricultural tool-making and maintenance.

(3) TBBC works through the Camp Committee in distributing food, shelter and non-food items such as cooking fuels, construction materials and basic livelihood tools. TBBC implements similar services as in Mae La Refugee Camp.

Mae La Temporary Shelter

In Mae La shelter, there are 23 agencies working directly and indirectly with UNHCR. These include ten organisations that receive funds with UNHCR and provide direct support to displaced persons, and 13 NGOs that are directly or indirectly involved in coordinating the discussions, the decision-making processes on delegated funds and in providing guidance.

NGOs oversee the shelter environment in Mae La camp. There are three NGOs involved in environmental management: the Catholic Office for Emergency Relief and Refugees (COERR), SOLIDARITIES and the Thai Burma Border Consortium (TBBC).

(1) COERR manages waste and camp environmental. Its main roles and responsibilities are (a) to oversee the entire waste management system e.g. household and waterways waste collection, waste disposal as well as organising environmental campaigns to raise awareness and knowledge on environmental protection; (b) to resolve issues regarding environmental and livelihood conflicts between the displaced persons within the camp and the host communities e.g. common usage of the river or collection of bamboo and leaves, resulting in negative image of the displaced persons and negative attitudes towards the displaced persons; and (c) to provide agricultural training to the displaced persons for future livelihood and general knowledge on crops planting
(2) In the Mae La camp, SOLIDARITIES carries out a water supply program, providing drinking water treatment and analysis. SOLIDARITIES took over this program from AMI in November 2008. SOLIDARITIES also works to improve access to sanitation facilities in the shelter. It monitors carriers of water-borne diseases, improves drainage in the area, has built 400 latrines and maintains 800 latrines, takes care of disinfection and is involved in the building of sewage disposal systems. Furthermore it tries to increase hygiene awareness by delivering hygiene training sessions, the distribution of hygiene kits, and prevention of and intervention during epidemics. Apart from these, SOLIDARITIES also works to improve access to drinking water. It protects and improves water resources; develops and maintains an existing water network, 63 public wells and pumping systems; develops water tapping systems and reservoirs; has built 1,000 m of drains; implements eight projects aimed at reinforcing ground soil in order to avoid stagnant water, which is a main carrier of disease; treats water and monitors the quality; is setting up a coordinating platform to manage water in the entire river basin; has established a model of the watershed; and promotes the planting of trees to reduce soil erosion. SOLIDARITIES also looks beyond the borders of the shelter. In October 2008 it started a 3 year project aimed at improving the living conditions for displaced persons and host villages along the Mae Ork Pha Roo River with a total number of beneficiaries of 50,000 people
(3) TBBC provides food, shelter and essential non-food items such as cooking fuel and building materials to the displaced people from Burma. It provides support for camp management through the refugee committees. The cooking fuel is made from sawmills waste, bamboo and coconut by-products and, where possible, the building materials are supplied from commercially grown plots. TBBC is dedicated to improving environmental conditions around the river; development of fish farming and micro-irrigation techniques, agricultural training sessions, setting up a fish breeding centre, and the rehabilitation of irrigation infrastructure (Table E.3).

Table E.3 List of the NGOs providing support in Mae La temporary shelter

No.	Name of organisation	Roles/responsibilities
1	Aide Medicale International (AMI)	- Water management, health and medical care
2	American Refugee Committee (ARC)	- SGBV training
3	Catholic Office for Emergency Relief and Refugees (COERR)	- Waste and environmental management - Sanitation and relief emergency
4	Handicap International (HI)	- Prosthetic limbs and landmine awareness education
5	International Refugee Committee (IRC)	- Refugees rights
6	Ministry of Education (MOE)	- Basic Thai education
7	Ministry of Interior (MOI)	- Administrative and security management of refugee camps - Assist National Security Council in screening and verifying refugee status
8	Right to Play (RTP)	- Child development through sports activities in Mae la camp since April 2008
9	Shanti Volunteer Association (SVA)	- Library services and socio-cultural activities - Manages six libraries within the camp area
10	Zuid Oost Azie Refugee Care, the Netherlands (ZOA)	- Livelihood and education training
Operational Partners—13 agencies		
1	Ruam Mit Foundation for the youths (DARE)	- Drugs, alcohol and HIV control programme
2	International Organisation for Migration (IOM)	-
3	Medicins Sans Frantiers (MSF)	- TB Control and clinical services
4	Overseas Processing Entity (OPE)	- Refugee screening and information gathering for DHS
5	Planned Parenthood Association of Thailand (PPAT)	- Reproductive health education
6	Shoklo Malaria Research Unit (SMRU)	- HIV awareness education, malaria control and pre-/post natal care for displaced persons and migrants
7	Thai Burma Border Commission (TBBC)	- Ensures sufficient food and housing supplies through the camp committee as well as building capacity for camp caretakers in managing different aspects of the camp
8	Taipei Overseas Peace Service (TOPS)	- Promote and provide education to children within the camp
9	Would Education/ Consortium (WE/ C)	- Build capacity and provide opportunities for the displaced persons
10	Adventist Development and Relief AgencyThailand (ANDRA)	- Education
11	Internationaal Christelijk Steunfonds Asia (ICS)	- Provision of educational materials
12	Solidarities International	- Sanitation and water management
13	Women's Education for Advancement and Empowerment (WEAVE)	- Vocational training for women

Source The authors

In addition to the above, there are 13 Karen-based social services agencies working within the shelter to promote social, cultural and quality of life for the displaced persons. These are:

(1) ACCS provides counseling for students wishing to pursue higher education beyond grade 10 within the camp or in Myanmar. Funding is provided by KNU.
(2) Eden Valley Academy (EVA) provides primary and secondary education certified by the PTO academy. Most funding is provided by AUSAID and partly from the tuition fee.
(3) Further Studies Programme (FSP) provides educational opportunities for students that completed grade 10 with higher education.
(4) Jury's Child Care Foundation assist children that have been impacted by conflicts e.g. Orphans, handicap children and child care for working parents. Funding is mostly provided from overseas.
(5) Karen Youth Organisation (Maela) runs by a Karen youth group that organises extra-curriculum activities in order to promote Karen culture and strengthening relationships with other people groups. Funding is providing mainly by NGOs and Karen Committee.
(6) Karen Women Organisation (KWO) implements women-related activities e.g. assist rape victims, promoting gender equality and capacity building for women's groups. Funding is mainly from NGOs such as TBBC, COERR, WEAVE as well as UNHCR in assisting the marketing of handmade Karen products overseas.
(7) KKBBSC provides theological education for Karens living within the shelters along the border areas as well as Thai Karen. Funding is provided mainly from Christian mission organisations as well as Karens living overseas.
(8) Leadership Management (LCM) promotes social awareness and responsibilities among youth. Funding was originally from Maier Mission Center (MMC) but later from other organisations when MMC ceased funding.
(9) MSF Mae La Hospital provides primary health care and patients care for displaced persons within the shelter as well as migrants from outside the shelter. This is funded by MSF.
(10) No.1 High School provides quality education to Karen children and youth in order to propagate Karen's traditions and culture. Funding is mainly from Consortium ZOA and students' tuition fee.
(11) No.4 Middle School (Muslim School) provides educational opportunities for students impacted by conflicts and for Muslim students. Funding is provided mainly from ZOA and Consortium.
(12) SMRU Clinic (Maela Zone B) provides malaria control and care for malaria patients residing within the camp as well as those along Thai–Myanmar border. Funding is provided by SMRU.

(13) Thisisandar Baddish Monastery is a Buddhist temple within the camp, promoting religious, Karen art and culture activities as well as basic education for youth in Myanmar, Karen and Sanskrit languages. Funding is mainly from NGOs and donations.

Summary of NGOs and Support for Displaced People's Settlements

Among the three locations studied, Mae La camp covers the largest camp area as well as being the most populated, this gave rise to the higher number of NGOs working in the area compare to other camp sites. It could be said that supports from NGOs have been the backbone of refugee camps management. Most NGOs working in the area of environmental protection do have the same roles and responsibilities in different camp sites. However, some agencies may only work in one area e.g. Solidarities International works in Mae La camp in partnership with CBOs in the area (Table E.4).

Host and Local Government Presence

Ban Tham Hin

There are camp security volunteers within the camp. There are village heads according to different zoning.

Ban Nai Soi

MOI maintains ultimate authority over the refugee camp. There are two levels of local camp government within the camp (1) CampCommittee—being the coordinating body with government authorities and other NGOs, (2) Zone

Table E.4 NGOs working in the area of environmental protection in the three temporary shelters

No.	Environmental issues	Ban Mae La	Ban Nai Soi	Ban Thum Hin
1	Waste management	COERR	IRC	IRC
2	Sanitation and water management	AMI SOLIDARITIES	IRC	IRC
3	Food, shelter and non-food items	TBBC	TBBC	TBBC
4	Environmental protection campaigns	COERR	COERR	COERR

Source The authors

village heads with 12 different zones and 1 village head per zone. There are 70 security volunteers in this camp.

Mae La

MOI maintains ultimate authority over the refugee camp. Tha Song Yang District officer, enforces refugee policy and controls the day-to-day running of the camps under the command of District Chief and there are Royal Thai Army Paramilitary Rangers in 4 check points.

Camp Committees are the administrative and management bodies of within refugee camps with a 3 year term and comprised 15 elected members. Management responsibilities are further delegated to the sub-committees or Community-based Organisations (CBOs) into different areas e.g. education, health, supplies, camp affairs and security issues, etc. Current Camp Committees have been elected in 2008. There are currently 25 members in the special security squad with sub-zone committees and village heads from zone A to C.

Outside the camp area, a central refugees committee (KRC) has been appointed to oversee and manage all seven refugee camps in Thailand. Each camp committee must regularly report camp issues to KRC. KRC plays the role of the coordinating body among RTG, donors, international/national agencies, foundations and camp committees.

Chulalongkorn University

Chulalongkorn University, Thailand's first institution of higher education, officially came into being in March 1917. The groundwork and preparation for it in terms of planning and development, however, took place more than a century ago. The worldwide economic, social and political changes in the late nineteenth century contributed to Siam's decision to adapt herself in order to avoid conflict with the Western powers ('Siam' became 'Thailand' in the year 1939). Thus the royal policy of King Chulalongkorn (Rama V) was to strengthen and improve government so that the country could successfully resist the tide of colonialism. One of the major parts of the policy, which would later prove to be deep-rooted and highly effective, was to improve the Siamese educational system so as to produce capable personnel to work in both the public and private sectors. As a result, a school was founded in 1871 at the Royal Pages' Barracks within the Grand Palace compound.

The development of Chulalongkorn University continued. From 1934 to 1958, the university emphasized the improvement of undergraduate education, and more faculties were established. In 1961 the university set up the Graduate School to be

S. Thadaniti and S. Chantavanich (eds.), *The Impact of Displaced People's Temporary Shelters on Their Surrounding Environment*, SpringerBriefs in Environment, Security, Development and Peace 16, DOI: 10.1007/978-3-319-02842-2,

responsible for graduate-level education. From 1962 till the present, the university has focused on graduate education and has set up research centres and institutes. The University, known familiarly as 'Chula', has grown constantly in the near-century since its founding.

At present Chulalongkorn University is composed of 19 faculties, 23 colleges and 17 research institutes. Currently there are over 38,000 students including 24,951 undergraduates, 13,391 postgraduates (10,881 on the Master's Degree and 2,150 on the Doctoral Degree programmes) and 2,800 faculty members. Its 87 international programmes have enjoyed a long and deserved high reputation for all-round academic attainment.

According to many Asian university rankings, Chulalongkorn University is Thailand's highest-ranked institution, with the highest scores in many subjects including Arts and Humanities, Social Sciences and Management, Natural Sciences, Engineering and Technology, and Life Sciences and Medicine.

Chulalongkorn University's Strategy 2012–2016 has been undertaken to formulate guidelines for the university's development plan. The initiative focuses on different aspects of development and improvement with the objective of raising the university to a level of excellence that will qualify it as a *World Class National University* and as the *Pillar of the Kingdom*.

The Institute of Asian Studies (IAS)

INSTITUTE OF ASIAN STUDIES
CHULALONGKORN UNIVERSITY

The Institute of Asian Studies (IAS) is an interdisciplinary research, teaching and service organization. IAS was established in 1967 as a unit within the Faculty of Political Science at Chulalongkorn University. After a considerable expansion of activities at IAS in 1979, an upgrade in the Institute's status was determined to be necessary. Consequently, on 10 May 1985, IAS was officially recognized as a separate institute at Chulalongkorn University, granting IAS a status equivalent to that of a faculty at the university.

Today, the strategic vision for IAS is to continue to serve the Thai community and the Asian region as a source of knowledge and expertise for a broad range of subject areas in the region including economic, social, political, and security concerns. This has been accomplished through the diligence and cooperation of a team of highly-qualified researchers who possess specialized knowledge about each country and subregion within Asia.

S. Thadaniti and S. Chantavanich (eds.), *The Impact of Displaced People's Temporary Shelters on Their Surrounding Environment*, SpringerBriefs in Environment, Security, Development and Peace 16, DOI: 10.1007/978-3-319-02842-2,

Asian Research Center for Migration

The Asian Research Center for Migration, based at the Institute of Asian Studies of Chulalongkorn University, is an internationally recognized centre of excellence in social science research. Located on the historic campus of Chulalongkorn University in the heart of Bangkok, ARCM is an important contributor to the research output of Thailand's oldest and most respected institution of higher learning, conducting critical policy-relevant research on international migration into, out of and within the South East Asian Region.

History

ARCM was initially founded in 1987 as the Indo-Chinese Refugee Information Center. The Center was established with the mission of conducting research on the flows of refugees from Cambodia, Laos, Vietnam and other South East Asian countries seeking asylum in Thailand. After the Indo-Chinese refugee crisis had abated in Thailand and the refugee camps were closed under the Comprehensive Plan of Action, the Center began to conduct research on new refugee situations that had begun to emerge in South East Asia.

In recognition of this newly broadened research focus, the Center was reconstituted as the Asian Research Center for Migration in 1995. Since that time,

S. Thadaniti and S. Chantavanich (eds.), *The Impact of Displaced People's Temporary Shelters on Their Surrounding Environment*, SpringerBriefs in Environment, Security, Development and Peace 16, DOI: 10.1007/978-3-319-02842-2,

the thematic areas of ARCM's research have expanded significantly and now include projects on all forms of international migration in South East Asia with a particular emphasis on Thailand as a sending, receiving and transit country.

Research Activities

Through published research, statistical data, consultation and policy recommendations related to cross-border migration in the South East Asia Region, the objective of ARCM's research activity is to support evidenced-based decision-making by governments, international agencies, and private sector organizations on migration-related issues. These activities are conducted by a multidisciplinary team of committed researchers, including both Thai and international experts, with backgrounds in a diverse range of academic fields relevant to migration such as sociology, anthropology, political science, economics and law.

About the Editors

Dr. Suwattana Thadaniti (Thailand) is an Associate Professor in Urban and Environmental Planning, Faculty of Architecture at Kasetsart University, Bangkok and an Advisor to the Chulalongkorn University's Social Research Institute (CUSRI) where she was Director during 2003–2007. She is also the Associate Director of the Master Degree Program in Human and Social Development of the Chulalongkorn University Graduate School. She has also worked as a Consultant to Department of Public Works and Town and Country Planning, Ministry of Interior where she was responsible for Community and District Planning of the Central Region of Thailand.

Her research focuses on Strategic Area Development Approaches for Implementing Metropolitan Development, Comprehensive Planning for Urban Development, Rehabilitation Planning for Community Environment and Settlement Development in the Tsunami Disaster Area, Urban Residential Development Planning, the Impact of Displaced People's Temporary Shelters on Their Surrounding Environment, and the Environment Assessment of Transborder Road Link (Dawei-Phu Nam Ron). Associate Professor Suwattana Thadaniti got her Ph.D. in Urban and Regional Planning from Technical University of Cracow, Poland.

Address: Dr. Suwattana Thadaniti, Social Research Institute, Chulalongkorn University Phayathai road, Bangkok 10330, Thailand.

Email: tsuwattana@yahoo.com

Website: www.cusri.chula.ac.th

S. Thadaniti and S. Chantavanich (eds.), *The Impact of Displaced People's Temporary Shelters on Their Surrounding Environment*, SpringerBriefs in Environment, Security, Development and Peace 16, DOI: 10.1007/978-3-319-02842-2,

Supang Chantavanich (Thailand) is a professor emeritus at the Faculty of Political Science, Chulalongkorn University. She is also the director of the Asian Research Center for Migration (ARCM) within the Institute of Asian Studies at Chula. During 2010–2011, she cooperated with UNDP to lead the research project *Sustainable Solutions to the Displaced Person Situation on the Thai–Myanmar Border* with EU funding. The project covered six studies of situational and policy analyses of displaced persons along the western borders in Thailand. The studies are finally revised into *Springer Briefs in Environment, Security, Development and Peace (ESDP)*, Volumes 15, 16, 17 and 18.

After she graduated in Sociology from the University of Grenoble, France, Supang Chantavanich focused her teaching and research areas on South East Asian society and culture, sociological theories, qualitative research, migration and development, the overseas Chinese, education and healthcare of migrant people, and labour migration and forced migration including refugee and human trafficking. Recently, she led a research team at ARCM which conducted a study of migrant fishermen from Myanmar and Cambodia in Thailand with the International Labour Organization. Another regional study on "Politics, Governance, Experience and Response to Flooding from the Locals' and Migrants' Perspective in ASEAN" is currently being conducted with researchers from eight ASEAN countries. The study addresses human security and conflicts among people affected by floods in the region.

Address: Prof: Supang Chantavanich, Asian Research Centre for Migration, Institute of Asian Studies, Chulalongkorn University, Phayathai road, Bangkok 10330, Thailand.

Email: supang.c@chula.ac.th

Website: http://arcmthailand.com

About the Other Authors

Dr. Bart Lambregts (The Netherlands) is a post-doc researcher at the Amsterdam Institute for Social Science Research (AISSR) of the University of Amsterdam and lecturer at the Division of Urban and Environmental Planning of Kasetsart University in Bangkok. He obtained his MSc. from Delft University of Technology (Civil Engineering) in 1995 and since then has worked for Witteveen+Bos Consulting Engineers, the OTB Research Institute for Housing, Urban and Mobility Studies, and, since 2003, the University of Amsterdam where he received his PhD (Human Geography). His main research interest concerns the role of advanced producer services industries in processes of globalization and local/regional development. In addition to that he has a keen interest in various sustainable urban development issues, including sustainable urban mobility, urban land use management and resilience in relation to climate change and flood threats. He has lectured on various courses on urban planning, transport planning, and economic geography. He currently lives in Bangkok, Thailand.

Address: Dr. Bart Lambregts, Division of Urban and Environmental Planning, Faculty of Architecture, Kasetsart University Phaho Yothin Road 10900 Bangkok, Thailand.

Email: B.Lambregts@uva.nl

Website: http://www.arch.ku.ac.th/uep/home.html.

S. Thadaniti and S. Chantavanich (eds.), *The Impact of Displaced People's Temporary Shelters on Their Surrounding Environment*, SpringerBriefs in Environment, Security, Development and Peace 16, DOI: 10.1007/978-3-319-02842-2,

Kanokphan U-sha (Thailand) is a Senior Researcher at the Institute of Asian Studies, Chulalongkorn University, where she researches and teaches Indian studies and supervises research on human and social development in Asia within the Master of Arts Programme in Human and Social Development.

Kanokphanholds a B.A. (Political Science) from Ramkhamhaeng University, and an M.A. (Sociology and Anthropology) from Chulalongkorn University. Her academic interests focus on globalization and social movement, comparative community development, and cultural anthropology studies between Thailand and India. She has conducted research projects on urbanization development, and several social impact assessments, Free Trade Area (FTA) Thailand–India, and environment, migration and disaster management.

Address: Ms. Kanokphan U-sha, Institute of Asian Studies, Chulalongkorn University, Phayathai road, Bangkok 10330, Thailand.

Email: kanokphan.u@chula.ac.th

Website: http://www.ias.chula.ac.th.

Saowanee Wijitkosum (Thailand) is a Lecturer, Researcher, and environmental and tourism specialist. She has served as Deputy Director of Chula Unisearch, Chulalongkorn University and on the Research Committee for Curriculum Administration for Graduate and Doctoral Programmes in the Environmental Sciences Programme and the Climate Change Cluster Committee at Chulalongkorn University. Her research interests and expertise include an environmental impact assessment of desertification; desertification risk assessment; water resource management; using GIS and RS for evaluation of the impacts of spatial land use on soil loss; land use planning and development; sustainable tourism management etc.

Address: Ms. Saowanee Wijitkosum, Environmental Research Institute, Chulalongkorn University, Bangkok, Thailand.

Email: w.m.saowanee@gmail.com

Website: www.eric.chula.ac.th.

Jaturapat Bhiromkaew (Thailand) is a Deputy Superintendent of Interpol and Foreign Relations Region 1 (ASEAN). His research interests focus on land use and transportation and travel behavior. He has had experience in many positions such as an Aide to the Deputy Commissioner General; Traffic Inspector; Chief Inspector of Tourist Police; Crime Suppression Inspector; Aide to the Commissioner of the Provincial Police; Inquiry Deputy Inspector; Deputy Inspector of the Human Resource Division etc. He has also had experience in working with the Hillsboro Police Department, Oregon, USA as a Professional Consultant in a research project on the demand for police services. He, additionally, did his intern with the High Tech Team in investigation of computer crimes. He received his Ph.D. in Urban Studies and Planning: Regional Science, from Portland State University, Oregon, USA.

Address: Dr. Jaturapat Bhiromkaew, Royal Thai Police, Bangkok, Thailand.
Email: patt_8@hotmail.com
Website: www.royalthaipolice.go.th.

Vollop Prombang (Thailand) is a Gp Capt. of the Royal Thai survey department. His area of expertise is on Cartographics, GIS and Terrain Analysis. He also worked with the Royal Thai Survey Department in many projects, eg. "Thai-Lao Boundary Survey Project" (2001), "Mae-Kong River Survey Project" (2003). He also made the surveying and physical data for town and country plans. He was in a research team on "Sustainable Solutions to the Displaced Person Situation on the Thai-Myanmar Border" with EU funding. At present, he is a general Manager of the surveying and mapping company "Peach and Paint Co. Ltd", Thailand.

Address: Gp Capt. Vollop Prombang, Peach and Paint Co. Ltd, Thailand.

Suchaow Toommakorn (Thailand) is an architect and designer of Pisut Technology Consultant Company. He received his Master Degree in Urban Design at the Faculty of Architecture, Chulalongkorn University and Bachelor Degree from the Faculty of Architecture, Urban Design and Creative Art, Mahasarakam Province, (Thailand). He was the associate researcher in the Jointed Team between Thammasart University, Chulalongkorn University and Massachusetts Institute of Technology that conducted the research on the settlement in the area of World Heritage of Sukhothai Province (2007). He has been the guest lecturer in some well known universities. In 2010, Suchaow Toommakorn won the second prize in the Design Award on the Project of land Development. His latest research is on the community plans at District level, funded by Development of Public Works and Town Planning.

About this Book

This book presents an overview of environmental issues and impacts associated with temporary shelters for displaced people along the Thai–Myanmar border, and offers recommendations to improve the environmental conditions in and around the settlements. Out of nine such temporary shelters, three were selected for detailed study: Ban Tham Hin (Ratchburi province), Ban Mai Nai Soi (Mae Hong Son province) and Ban Mae La (Tak province). In each of these shelters a variety of research methods was used to assess the environmental conditions, analyse ways of living and use of resources by displaced persons, and disclose their perceptions of the environmental conditions they face. Efforts were also made to assess the environmental impacts produced by the presence of the shelters on the surrounding areas, including listening to officials and representatives from these areas in focus group meetings and through interviews. This book provides practical and realistic recommendations for policy options to reach a durable solution for refugees at the borders. Practitioners and policymakers from governments, international organizations and international NGOs will benefit from the findings and recommendations proposed in this book. The volume is also helpful for those who study forced migration and its denouement in the age of globalization.

S. Thadaniti and S. Chantavanich (eds.), *The Impact of Displaced People's Temporary Shelters on Their Surrounding Environment*, SpringerBriefs in Environment, Security, Development and Peace 16, DOI: 10.1007/978-3-319-02842-2,

MIX
Papier aus verantwortungsvollen Quellen
Paper from responsible sources
FSC® C105338

If you have any concerns about our products,
you can contact us on
ProductSafety@springernature.com

In case Publisher is established outside the EU,
the EU authorized representative is:
Springer Nature Customer Service Center GmbH
Europaplatz 3, 69115 Heidelberg, Germany

Printed by Libri Plureos GmbH
in Hamburg, Germany